How to Wake Up

A Buddhist-Inspired Guide
to Navigating Joy and Sorrow

Toni Bernhard

WISDOM PUBLICATIONS · BOSTON

Wisdom Publications
199 Elm Street
Somerville, MA 02144 USA
www.wisdompubs.org

Library of Congress Cataloging-in-Publication Data
Bernhard, Toni.
 How to wake up : a Buddhist-inspired guide to navigating joy and sorrow /
Toni Bernhard.
    pages cm
  Includes index.
  ISBN 1-61429-056-3 (pbk. : alk. paper)
  1. Religious life—Buddhism. I. Title.
  BQ5395.B47 2013
  294.3'444—dc23

                          2013000338

ISBN 978-1-61429-056-8; eBook ISBN 978-1-61429-067-4

17 16 15 14 13
5 4 3 2 1

Cover design by Phil Pascuzzo. Interior design by Gopa&Ted2. Set in Sabon Lt
Std 10.8/16.

Wisdom Publications' books are printed on acid-free paper and meet the guidelines for permanence and durability of the Production Guidelines for Book Lon-
gevity of the Council on Library Resources.

Printed in the United States of America.

This book was produced with environmental mindfulness. We have elected to print this title on 30% PCW
recycled paper. As a result, we have saved the following resources: 19 trees, 9
million BTUs of energy, 1,595 lbs. of greenhouse gases, 8,647 gallons of water,
and 579 lbs. of solid waste. For more information, please visit our website, www
.wisdompubs.org. This paper is also FSC® certified. For more information,
please visit www.fscus.org.

For my granddaughters Malia and Camden with all my love . . .

May your joys be many.
May you meet sorrow with compassion.
May you find peace and contentment.
May you become buddhas.

Table of Contents

Introduction

Ten Thousand Joys, Ten Thousand Sorrows

It is exactly because the Buddha was a human being
that countless buddhas are possible.
—THICH NHAT HANH

THE TITLE of this introduction—ten thousand joys, ten thousand sorrows—is attributed to the fourth-century BCE Taoist sage Chuang Tzū. The number *ten thousand* stands for unlimited. The phrase points to the seemingly countless joys and sorrows in everyone's life—how it's easy at times and difficult at times, fulfilling at times and frustrating at times, happy at times and sad at times. Life is a mixture of pleasant and unpleasant experiences, of pleasure and pain—physically, mentally, and emotionally.

The Buddha's life also had its joys and sorrows. Despite those sorrows, he became "the awakened one" (which is what the word *buddha* means). As I understand the Buddha's teachings, every moment that we engage our life fully as it is, we have the potential to awaken to a peace and well-being that are not dependent on whether a particular experience is joyful or sorrowful. Moreover, each moment is followed, in the blink of an eye, by another moment in which awakening is possible.

I don't believe there was anything supernatural about the Buddha's awakening. After meditating for seven days and nights under a fig tree and carefully observing his experience, he *woke up* to what it means to be human—both its stark realities and the potential it holds for us to find peace and contentment.

Building on this insight, he left us detailed instructions for awakening. These instructions can be found in his teachings on wisdom, mindfulness, and open-heartedness. They are the three subjects of this book. The path of awakening is available to all of us, no matter what our religious or metaphysical beliefs are and no matter how difficult our circumstances may be.

In my own life, it has been the difficulties and struggles that motivated me to look deeply at the Buddha's teachings on awakening in order to find some measure of peace and contentment. Since 2001, the most challenging difficulty I've faced is chronic illness. In the summer of 2001, I had the next twenty years of my life planned. I'd be teaching law at the University of California at Davis, as I'd already been doing for almost twenty years. I'd continue to be active in the life of a boy in Child Protective Services for whom I'd been appointed as mentor. I'd travel to visit my children and their families. And I'd attend as many Buddhist meditation retreats as I could.

Suddenly, everything changed. My husband Tony (yes, Tony!) and I took a trip to Paris. On the second day there, I got sick with what was initially diagnosed as an acute viral infection. But I never recovered, and I was forced to trade the classroom for the bedroom. In addition to leaving my profession, I had to give up the mentoring, the traveling, the retreat practice. At the time, it broke my heart.

During the first few years of being housebound, I lived in what

I can only describe as a state of shock. I couldn't believe I wasn't getting better. I blamed myself for not recovering, certain that my illness was proof of a defect in my character. And I desperately longed for the life I'd been used to.

Gradually, though, I came to see that my unremitting desire for the life I could no longer lead and the blame I was directing at myself were only adding more suffering, in the form of stress and anguish, to the physical suffering of the illness. Inspired by the Buddha—whose teachings were waiting in the wings for me to return to—I decided to treat the illness as my starting point and begin to build a new life.

From my bed, I wrote *How to Be Sick: A Buddhist-Inspired Guide for the Chronically Ill and Their Caregivers*, hoping it would point the way for those living with chronic pain and illness to find a measure of peace despite their health challenges. But something unexpected happened after the book's release. I began to get "thank you" emails and notes from people who were perfectly healthy. For them, illness was serving as a metaphor for whatever difficulties they were facing in life: stress on the job or at school; tension in a relationship; sadness over a loss or separation; worry stemming from parental or other caregiver responsibilities; struggles due to aging; anxiety over money; and sometimes just the challenge of getting through the day. I learned from their emails and notes how long the list of life's ten thousand sorrows can be.

That feedback encouraged me to write this second book, with the purpose of exploring how our difficulties and struggles can be the very seeds of awakening to what the Buddha discovered. The Buddha wasn't concerned with heaven or hell, with miracles or saints. He avoided metaphysical speculation altogether. He was interested in investigating the human condition, particularly the presence of suffering in our lives and how we might alleviate it so that we can find the peace and well-being we all hope for. He left us dozens of concrete practices to help with this, and I share my understanding of many of them in this book.

Each chapter in the book includes practices that have helped me integrate the Buddha's teachings into my daily life. As I work with a practice myself, I often take notes on my experience. Putting my thoughts in writing forces me to articulate more clearly what I am learning and this helps me lay down new habits. The Buddha said this about practice: "Whatever a person frequently thinks and ponders upon, that becomes the inclination of his mind . . . "

Inclination is the key word here. For example, each time our "thinking and pondering" gives rise to compassionate thought or compassionate action, our inclination to be compassionate is strengthened, making it more likely that we'll behave compassionately in the future. We're, in effect, planting a behavioral seed that can grow into a habit. We are forming our character.

And so, whenever we practice cultivating wisdom, mindfulness, and open-heartedness—the latter referring to four psychological states, including compassion and equanimity—we are turning ourselves into a person who is wise, mindful, and open-hearted. The implications of this can be life-changing. It means that we have the ability to change ourselves no matter how ingrained our painful mental habits have become. Neuroscientists are finding this to be true—that our brains are constantly rewiring and reconditioning themselves based on our thoughts, speech, and actions. But the Buddha knew this long ago.

People who are new to the Buddha's teachings often think there is one entity: *Buddhism.* But there are dozens of traditions, including Theravadin, Tibetan, Zen, Pure Land, Nichiren, and the more recent Secular Buddhism. They've been forming and evolving for thousands of years, and the tenets of one tradition aren't always consistent with the tenets of another. Some people consider Buddhism to be a religion, others see it as a spiritual practice, and still others as a philosophy of life. I think of the Buddha as a master psychologist because he understood the human condition, including how our thoughts, speech, and actions can intensify our suffering and how we can find relief from that suffering.

From over twenty years of immersion in his teachings, it is my experience that when we fully engage what's happening in the moment, the conditions arise for awakening. The Buddha's teachings are not passive. Engaging life challenges us to be fully present and actively involved in our moment-to-moment experience, without clinging to joy and without resisting sorrow.

To *wake up*, we have to investigate and learn for ourselves what gives rise to suffering and unhappiness in our lives and what we can do to find peace and well-being. The Buddha laid out a path for us to follow, but we have to do the work. I hope this book makes walking that path a bit easier.

Cultivating Wisdom

I

Change, Change, Change

*That nothing is static or fixed, that all is fleeting and
impermanent, is the first mark of existence. It is the ordinary
state of affairs. Everything is in process. Everything—every
tree, every blade of grass, all the animals, insects, human
beings, buildings, the animate and the inanimate—is always
changing, moment to moment.*

—PEMA CHÖDRÖN

WE EMBARK ON the path of awakening by cultivating wisdom. In Buddhist philosophy, wisdom refers to seeing things clearly just the way they are so we're less likely to be deluded or confused about what to expect in life. The Buddha woke up to the reality of the human condition, specifically that all human beings have three life experiences in common: we are subject to impermanence and change; we cannot find a fixed, unchanging self; and we will encounter suffering.

These three experiences are interrelated. If we truly and deeply come to understand one of them, we'll understand the other two better as well. In this section of the book—cultivating wisdom—we'll investigate these *three marks of experience* (what the Tibetan Buddhist teacher Pema Chödrön refers to above as marks of existence).

We'll begin with impermanence and change. Subsequent chapters will cover the other two marks—no-fixed-self and suffering. In the last chapter in this section, we'll look at five habits of mind—called hindrances—that are obstacles on the path of awakening because they cloud our ability to see clearly the three marks of experience.

Impermanence and Change

Scientific and religious traditions are in agreement that impermanence, change, and the uncertainty they imply are experiences common to all human beings. The Buddha wanted to be sure we understood the radical implications of this universal law. He put it this way: "Everything that arises has the nature to pass away." I would only add italics: *everything* that arises has the nature to pass away. The material world around us arises and passes away. Our thoughts and emotions arise and pass away. The Buddha's words also remind us that, having been born, we are subject to illness, old age, death, and separation from our loved ones. This can be a sobering fact—one we may not want to hear—but insisting that life is otherwise only increases our unhappiness and suffering when these events come to pass, as they inevitably will.

It's not difficult to understand the truth of impermanence intellectually, but it can be hard to see in our everyday experience. This is partly because we perceive that, for the most part, every day we see the same people, perform the same tasks, even have the same thoughts and emotions. This makes it appear that our lives are static and unchanging. But that's not the case.

For example, if you were unhappy about your job last month,

you may well be unhappy about it today, making it appear to you that you've experienced one month of static, unrelenting unhappiness. If you look carefully, though, change has been ever-present; your frustration was not a singular unchanging experience. Yes, there may have been days when you felt hopeless and depressed about your job. But there were also times when a coworker made you laugh, or you felt good about the quality of your work, or you had a moment of calm acceptance that the world of work is not always going to be pleasant. If you were to examine that past month carefully, you'd realize that even your unhappiness had its ups and downs. Whenever we look carefully, we see this is always the case: no thought or emotion truly remains static or recurs in exactly the same way.

The language we use can also make it hard to see impermanence in our everyday experience. We name the objects of our perception—Mt. Everest, cloud, daisy, chronic pain—and then tend to freeze them in our minds and come to think of them as discrete entities with an essence that defines them. Having done this, we lose sight of their ever-changing quality, whether that change takes place slowly (as with a mountain or chronic pain) or quickly (as with a wispy cloud or a flower).

Mindfulness Helps Us See Impermanence

We can work on increasing our awareness of the impermanent nature of our experience. This conscious awareness is called mindfulness. Mindfulness simply means paying careful attention to what is happening in the present moment. This careful attention makes it easier to recognize moment-to-moment change in the objects of our perception. We become acutely aware of how a drizzle briefly changes to rain and then back to a drizzle or how what appeared to be a solid block of pain in the body is, instead, a constantly changing mixture of tightness, softness, heat, cold, pulsations, and waves of more and less intense sensations. With mindfulness, we can also become aware that our unhappiness about our job from a month ago has a different feeling tone from our unhappiness about it today.

We can also see how conditions in every moment contribute to the arising of the next moment. Everything comes into being and subsequently changes as a result of the coming together of a particular constellation of conditions. The hot sun hitting a flower petal may—along with the amount of moisture in the ground—complete the conditions for the petal, in the next moment, to begin to change from pink to brown. A dog seeing a stranger coming up the walkway may—along with the dog's disposition—complete the conditions for the dog to change from an affectionate creature to a growling one.

With careful, practiced attention, we can become acutely aware of the impermanence of everything in the moment. Seneca, the first-century Roman philosopher, said to count each day as a separate life. In Buddhist philosophy, we go even further: every moment is a separate life. To me, this means that every moment is a fresh start. In the previous moment, we may have blamed ourselves for something, but in this moment, we can change that response to one of kindness and compassion toward ourselves. And if we miss that chance, the very next moment offers another fresh opportunity. Every moment holds the possibility of awakening to a feeling of peace and well-being.

Uncertainty and Unpredictability

We have a tendency to underestimate the impact of impermanence in our lives, especially how uncertainty and unpredictability are its hallmarks in our everyday experience. If you'd have asked me on May 21, 2001, the day before I got sick with the illness that continues to this day, "Do you believe that life is uncertain and unpredictable?" I would have said, "Of course!" And yet, despite years of immersion in the Buddha's teaching, on that twenty-first day of May in 2001, I now realize that I felt certain about many things, including:

- ‣ I'd be teaching for at least another fifteen years, and Tony and I would continue to take our treasured trips to Moloka'i where we'd rent the same secret hideaway I'd discovered in 1995.
- ‣ The large hackberry tree in our front yard that kept the blistering afternoon sun from hitting our house during California's hot Central Valley summers would be standing long after I no longer lived there.
- ‣ The World Trade Center towers would continue to dominate the New York City skyline, their image instantly identifying a movie or a television show as being set in the Big Apple.

I was wrong on every count.

These are three examples of how uncertainty and unpredictability can catch us by surprise even though they are ever-present in our lives. Fully engaging them with an open mind—our wisdom mind—is essential to our well-being because, when we recoil in aversion to life's uncertainty and unpredictability, our suffering over events that are already painful just intensifies.

That said, uncertainty and unpredictability can also be our friends. Buddhist teacher Joseph Goldstein likes to say: "Anything can happen at any time." This includes crises and horrific events, but it may also include the possibility of an improvement in health, a never-before-seen clear view of the sunset because of our treeless front yard, or even the sudden laying down of weapons by a terrorist group.

Impermanence and its corollaries—uncertainty and unpredictability—aren't confined to major life events. They permeate every aspect of our lives. If you were to make a list of how you thought the day ahead would unfold for you, and then, at the end of the day, reviewed that list, I'm confident there would be a notable discrepancy between the day you expected and the day that took place.

I tried this recently as a practice. The day I had planned looked like this:

1. See dentist at 9:10.
2. Come home and eat breakfast.
3. Work on book until noon and then nap.
4. Work on book from 2:30–4:00.
5. Eat dinner around 6:00 and get into bed at 7:30.

At the end of the day, I wrote a note about how the day actually unfolded:

After the dental work, my mouth was too numb to eat breakfast and I wasn't feeling well enough to work on my book. After my nap, I got set up for writing, but before I could start, Tony got home earlier than expected from a trip to Los Angeles and wanted to visit. By 4:00, I was too tired to work on the book. I asked to eat dinner early so I could get into bed by 6:30.

I hope you'll try this *uncertainty and unpredictability practice.* It's a good way to become aware of impermanence and its corollaries in your life. Although it may appear that each of our days is set and static, in truth, they are fluid and inconstant. All we can count on is that the present moment will be exactly as it is.

Living Skillfully with Uncertainty and Unpredictability

My friend Sandy has devised a practice to help her make peace with life's everyday uncertainty and unpredictability. Her idea is simple in theory, if not always easy to execute.

She treats interruptions as a normal part of her day. For example, if she's interrupted while practicing her cello, instead of getting irritated, she switches her attention to the new direction her day has taken. She told me that she's much more relaxed and at ease now that she's accepted that every day will be filled with uncertainty and unpredictability.

Sandy has two teenagers at home, so I figured, if she could do it, I could do it. I started small by picking activities that weren't important for me to finish right away. I tried her practice while washing dishes, composing an email, and watching a recorded TV show. Before I started each of these activities, I resolved that, if I were interrupted, I'd remind myself that being interrupted was to be expected. Then I'd switch my attention to the source of the interruption and greet it with welcoming curiosity instead of irritation.

I was sure that Sandy wasn't 100 percent successful, so I didn't hold myself to too high a standard. Still, I'd been doing very well with this practice—until I took it out into the world. One day during the writing of this book, Tony and I went to a local espresso place for a short outing, so I could work on a chapter in an environment other than my bedroom. I don't go out often, so every minute of time at this café was precious to me.

About five minutes after we sat down, I suddenly heard a warm "Hello!" I looked up from the paragraph I was concentrating on and there was the mother of a boy who'd been on my son's basketball team in high school. I'd only known her casually, but she struck up a conversation with Tony and me as if we were old friends.

I could feel aversion arising over this "interruption," as I thought, "Please—*please*—go away so I can get back to my writing." But she stayed. In a moment of rudeness, I picked up my pen and went back to the chapter at hand, leaving her standing next to our table, talking to Tony even though he knew her no better than I did.

With pen in hand, marking up a page, I suddenly remembered Sandy's practice. I put the pen down, turned and gave my full attention to our visitor. Within seconds, my aversion—and the suffering and stress that accompanied it—dropped away, to be replaced by genuine appreciation for the presence of another human being. It felt good to be fully engaging someone who was kind enough to stop at our table, instead of mentally pushing her away as an unwanted intrusion on the outing I had expected to turn out a certain way. We had a lovely conversation and, as she left, I only hoped she hadn't noticed my rudeness.

Whether impermanence appears to be friend or foe at the moment, seeing clearly into this universal truth can help us awaken to a peace and well-being that are not dependent on whether events turn out the way we expected them to. Upon getting up each morning, we can reflect on how we can't be certain if the day will unfold as we think it will and then resolve to greet it nonetheless with curiosity and wisdom. Greeting the day with curiosity means being interested in what each moment has to offer. And greeting it with wisdom means not turning away in aversion from our experience, even if it's unpleasant and even if it's not what we had hoped for.

Buddhist scholar John Peacock offers this contemporary translation of the Buddha's final words to his followers: "All things are impermanent—get on with it!" In those moments when we don't feel threatened by change and uncertainty, we're able to "get on with it" by engaging our life fully, however it unfolds. Peace and well-being are to be found in embracing, as it is, each fleeting moment.

2

Self as Ever-Shifting Flow

What we call "I" is just a swinging door which
moves when we inhale and when we exhale.
—SHUNRYU SUZUKI

IMPERMANENCE IS the first mark of experience common to all human beings. The second one is what Buddhists call *no-fixed-self*. Like uncertainty and unpredictability, no-fixed-self is a corollary of the universal law of impermanence. But unlike those two corollaries, no-fixed-self was a concept unique to the Buddha's teaching. He took the radical step of applying impermanence even to what we think of as our *self*. Twenty-five hundred years later, neuroscientists are coming to the same conclusion; they're finding multiple circuitry in the brain, but no fixed seat of the self. As Pema Chödrön noted in the quotation that begins the previous chapter, "nothing is static or fixed." That would include this notion of *self*.

This person I think of as a fixed entity, "Toni Bernhard," is, in reality, an ever-changing combination of physical traits, thoughts, emotions, and actions. Where, then, do I get the idea of "Toni

Bernhard"? As a result of past and current conditions in my life, this combination of physical traits, thoughts, emotions, and actions tends to come together in repeating patterns. The mind then abstracts from these patterns and assumes they make up an intrinsic someone called "Toni Bernhard." The mind, in effect, creates a story, starring a character it calls (drum roll, please . . .) *Toni Bernhard*! And so, I take that to be *who I am*—an entity with fixed, unchanging characteristics.

Here's an example. When I was a teenager, I behaved in repeating patterns that society had identified as signs of depression. Quite understandably, this led my family to come up with this abstraction from my behavior: I was a depressed person. As a result, I took on that label and that identity: "Toni Bernhard, depressed person." I thought that was *who I was*, and that "depressed person" was a fixed aspect of my being. But those emotional and behavioral patterns changed as soon as I moved out of the house to go to college. That notion of an intrinsic, fixed self—depressed person—turned out to be an illusion. It was just a passing identity based on the repetition of emotional and behavioral patterns in my life at the time.

Many years later, my idea of who I was became "law professor." As I'd done with "depressed person," now "law professor" became how I identified myself. When I unexpectedly had to stop working due to illness, the identity of "law professor" followed me from the classroom to the bedroom. Although I was clearly unable to carry out the duties of my profession, I would lie in bed and anxiously think, "If I'm not a law professor, who am I?"

It took me several years to see that clinging to the identity "law professor" had become a source of deep sorrow and suffering for me. It was then that I realized that "law professor" was an abstract idea, based on repeating patterns in my experience at the time: going to the same place every day where people called me "Professor Bernhard"; repeatedly seeing that very label in writing—on the name plate next to my office door, on my faculty mailbox, on written materials.

"Law professor" turned out not to be a fixed self any more than "depressed person" had been. Both were stories in my mind—abstractions from my experience that I clung to as an intrinsic quality of *me*. And even though the identity "depressed person" was one I *didn't* like and the identity "law professor" was one I *did*, in both instances, when I let go of those identities, I felt a great sense of peace and liberation.

In the same way, the identity "Toni Bernhard" is a story. Of course, it's a necessary one at times! After all, I can't get a driver's license unless I'm willing to say, "I am Toni Bernhard." And I'm using self-referential terms, such as "I" and "me," throughout this book in order to communicate effectively. But even so, I'm working to hold the identity "Toni Bernhard" lightly, without believing it implies a fixed, nonchanging essence.

The Many Ways We're Fixed in Identities

We humans are incredibly adept at identifying with our experiences and circumstances and then coming to assume they are part of who we are intrinsically. We can identify ourselves with a race, ethnic background, gender, and nationality. We can identify ourselves with a job title. We can identify with what we perceive to be our personality traits: smart, funny, trustworthy, stupid, judgmental, foolish. We can identify with our bodies: short, tall, fat, thin, handsome, unattractive, healthy, sick. We can identify with our religious affiliation or with our political leanings: "I *am* a liberal"; "I *am* a conservative."

Some of these identities are internalized during our formative years due to cultural influences or to how we were treated by others. As we repeatedly recall those influences and experiences, we come to believe that they represent real qualities of ourselves, and this can become a deep source of suffering. For example, if a parent repeatedly told us that we didn't try hard enough or that we were always in the way or that we couldn't do anything right, we're likely as adults to think of those characterizations as fixed qualities of ourselves—intrinsic to who we are. If this is the case for you, my heartfelt wish is that this chapter will help you see that you need not define yourself by any of these identities.

If you'd like to experiment with the ways in which you've created fixed identities, make a list of all the identities you've been using to define yourself. My list includes sick person, hard worker, devoted parent, worrier, perfectionist, author. When you're done with your list, reflect separately on each of the identities you've written down. Is it a source of joy for you? Suffering? A mixture of the two? Does it carry a judgment, meaning do you think of the identity as "good" or as "bad"? For example, if you listed "overweight" or "easily frustrated," a negative judgment might have arisen along with your self-characterization. If you listed "highly motivated" or "generous," you may have noticed a positive judgment arise: "It's good to be highly motivated"; "I'm proud that I'm generous."

Now begin to examine the effects of becoming attached to these identities. When I do this, two insights stand out for me. First, I notice that the identities that I judge negatively are sources of suffering for me. One example: the identity "sick person." It's a source of suffering because the identity brings along with it stressful thoughts and emotions: "I shouldn't be sick"; "I've been cheated out of a dozen years of my life"; "What if I get worse and worse?"

However, if I look more deeply at the identity "sick person," I see that it has no intrinsic existence. There is this body and there is this mind; there are physical sensations and mental sensations. There's no reason to label either one as the fixed identity "sick." In fact, there's a lot this body can do that so-called "not sick" people can do: walk, talk, eat, pet the dog. And so I practice looking at the phrase "sick person" as an abstraction in my mind, with no intrinsic existence. When I do this, I feel a sense of relief and freedom. There's just this moment—here, now—containing whatever physical and mental sensations I'm experiencing.

The second insight that stands out for me is that the identities on my list—even those I judge as "good"—make me feel separate from others. And when I look closely, I see that this is also a source of suffering for me. This sense of separation occurs because identities are often formed by comparing ourselves to others. If I think of myself as highly motivated, I'm separating myself from those whom I perceive not to be. The same would occur if I think of myself as generous. I've put myself into an identity box, so to speak, and then feel separated from those who I perceive don't fit in it. But aren't highly motivated people sometimes also not motivated? And aren't generous people sometimes also not so generous? I think so. Even identities we form around race, gender, religion, nationality, and political affiliation can make us feel separate from others.

I joke with Tony about a test I've devised for deciding if an identity is worth defining myself by. I ask: "Does the identity pass my hound-dog test?" I spend a lot of time with my hound dog Rusty, so I figure he knows the *real me*. Does he think of me as a Buddhist? No! An American? No! A published author? Certainly not! You get the idea. I hope you'll try this *no-fixed-identity exercise.*

One reason we seek the "real me" by holding on to these identities is that they provide us with a sense of security. But we know from the law of impermanence that there's not much security to be found in this life. And so I work on shedding the identities I've come to regard as "me" or "mine." Instead, I try to embrace the insecurity that comes from not being a fixed self at all.

Not Clinging to Identities Is Liberating

Thinking of myself as an ever-changing process rather than as a fixed person gives my life a feeling of fluidness and potential. In *Buddhism Without Beliefs*, Stephen Batchelor refers to himself as "an unfolding narrative." When I'm able to see that the words appearing to fix me in an unchanging identity are simply abstract concepts arising and passing in the mind, I'm able to stop clinging to the idea of a fixed self. Then I can let that narrative unfold, and possibilities open up that I may not have even imagined.

For example, it was only when I let go of the identity "law professor" that I was able to begin writing my first book. This was partly because when law professors engage in scholarly writing, they don't talk about their personal lives. And so when I was stuck in the identity "law professor," it never occurred to me that I could write a book in which I could use my personal experience with chronic illness to illustrate the points I was making.

My favorite description of no-fixed-self comes from the eco-philosopher Joanna Macy: "I am a flow-through of matter, energy, and information." I like to consciously think of myself (or, my "self") as nothing more than a constellation of causes and conditions that have come together at this particular moment in time. Indeed, many scholars think that this was what the Buddha was referring to when he talked about *rebirth*—rebirth moment-to-moment into ever-shifting identities, distinct from but related to the identities of previous moments. When I'm able to recognize that clinging to an identity is an attempt to freeze in time what is, in reality, part of the uninterrupted flow of life, I feel light and free.

It's important to understand that thinking in terms of no-fixed-self is not a kind of reductionism; it is not an attempt to explain away the complexities of existence by simply saying nothing abides. The concept of no-fixed-self is a pointer that is intended to inspire us to investigate the nature of the human condition. Why do we suffer? What can be done to alleviate it? How does the idea of a fixed self contribute to suffering and unhappiness?

Perhaps you think of yourself as an angry or impatient or judgmental person. The lesson of no-fixed-self is that you need not feel stuck in any of these identities. They've arisen as a result of repeating patterns of thoughts, emotions, and actions in your life, and such patterns can change. Using the practices in this book, you can begin to change the inclination to be angry or impatient or judgmental. Like all phenomena, these mental states are impermanent; they are not fixed characteristics.

Freedom comes from not clinging to any identity at all, whether we think of it as desirable or not. Not becoming attached to identities we perceive as undesirable—depressed person, for example—frees us to think of ourselves as multidimensional, as opposed to being limited to a few painful characteristics. And not becoming attached to identities we perceive as desirable—law professor, for example—frees us from the suffering that will arise when those identities yield, as they inevitably will, to the law of impermanence.

Far from being nihilistic, the truth of no-fixed-self opens our hearts and minds—our very lives—to possibilities we might not have imagined before!

3

Can't Get No Satisfaction

We must embrace pain and burn it
as fuel for our journey.
—KENJI MIYAZAWA

HAVING LOOKED AT the first two marks of experience—
impermanence and no-fixed-self—we now turn our attention
to exploring the third mark: suffering or dissatisfaction. It's inevitable that our lives will be a struggle at times. None of us are strangers
to stress, unease, suffering, and dissatisfaction. The Buddha was
well aware of this. The word he used to describe this experience is
dukkha.

Dukkha is usually translated as *suffering.* Suffering is an aspect
of dukkha, but it's too narrow in scope to explain this core Buddhist concept. Some Buddhist scholars say we should stop trying to
translate dukkha altogether and let this complex word enter, as is,
into the cultural stream in the West. I think of dukkha as the feeling
of dissatisfaction we experience with the circumstances of our lives.
This description encompasses the many words that are often used

to translate dukkha: suffering, stress, unease, anguish, discontent, and just plain unhappiness. As shorthand descriptions of dukkha, I'll mostly use the words *suffering* and *dissatisfaction*.

The Buddha didn't say that life is *only* dukkha. He understood that every life is a mixture of joy and sorrow. The written record of his oral teachings is full of stories about the Buddha and his followers enjoying themselves and even having a good laugh. But he wanted to focus our attention on dukkha because he knew that the first step in finding relief from it was to look it squarely in the eye and get to know it well. It's a relief to encounter a teacher who "tells it like it is" instead of sugarcoating the experience of being human.

Dukkha and the Cessation of Dukkha

The Buddha told his disciples many times: "I teach dukkha and the cessation of dukkha." This is a remarkable statement because it means that the path of awakening is inextricably tied to understanding how suffering and dissatisfaction operate in our lives, so we can begin the process of freeing ourselves from them.

It's important to recognize that "the cessation of dukkha" doesn't mean that we can put an end to life's unpleasant experiences. Bodies get sick and injured and grow old. In our emotional lives, we'll experience the grief of separation and loss. No one gets a pass on the ten thousand sorrows. By "the cessation of dukkha," the Buddha was referring to putting an end to the dissatisfaction we experience with our life however it happens to be at this moment.

Using emotions as an example, dukkha doesn't refer to the mere presence of an unpleasant emotion. It refers to our *dissatisfaction* with its presence. Dukkha arises when we resist a painful emotion instead of accepting that this is what we're feeling at the moment. Acknowledging the presence of an unpleasant experience is itself a moment of awakening because it's a moment of gracefully engaging our life as it is for us right now.

Our difficulties and struggles are the pain that the Japanese poet Kenji Miyazawa calls on us to embrace in the quotation that begins this chapter. This embrace is an opening of the heart that sets the stage for the arising of four open-hearted states of mind: kindness, compassion, appreciative joy, and equanimity. We'll be looking at these in detail later in the book. Freeing ourselves from dukkha is a tall order, but the Buddha left us many insights and practices—such as cultivating these open-hearted states—to help us with this task.

You Can't Always Get What You Want

When I first encountered the Buddha's teaching on suffering and dissatisfaction, instead of feeling disheartened, I felt understood. Here was someone offering an honest and straightforward description of how I felt at some point every day of my life, whether it was mild irritation over being put on hold on the phone, stress about an upcoming appointment, or anguish over my health. In addition to feeling relieved, I felt a profound connection to others. The circumstances of our lives may result in this suffering and dissatisfaction showing up for us with slightly different "flavors," but beneath the surface, we know what others' dukkha feels like because we experience it ourselves.

Reflect on your life at this moment. Aren't you, at least in some sense, dissatisfied with it? This dissatisfaction may show up as unease over the "big questions": Does my life have meaning? What does climate change mean for the future of the planet? It may be tied to the stresses of everyday life: tension in a relationship, stress on the job or at school, financial difficulties. It may be triggered by mundane discomforts and irritations: the dog barking next door, the lost sock in the dryer. Notice how there is an ongoing effort—

subtle or intense—to adjust the circumstances of your day-to-day life to be more to your liking.

When I think about what it would take for me not to be dissatisfied, it seems as if I'd have to arrange my life and the world to conform totally to my liking—and then have them stay that way:

- I would cease being sick and immediately travel to the ocean to body surf;
- My two grown children and their families would move in next door—one family on each side will do;
- The daytime temperature outside would range from 70–80 degrees Fahrenheit—always;
- Politicians on both side of the aisle would come to share my views;
- I would never be cranky again.

In other words, my happiness appears to be contingent on life always conforming to how I think it should be. But that's not going to happen. As the Buddhist monk Ajahn Brahm says of this state of mind: "You'd be asking the world for something it can never give you."

If we try to control all of life's circumstances, we'll be rife with dissatisfaction. The universal law of impermanence dictates that pleasant experiences won't last and unpleasant experiences will arise, often most unexpectedly. Trying to control the uncontrollable is a recipe for dukkha.

Before I became chronically ill, I expected to be teaching for at least another fifteen years. Working at the law school was a labor of love. The students learned from me and I learned from them. It was my dream job. And so when I failed to recover and it wasn't clear if I could continue teaching, I tried to control the circumstances of my life with a vengeance. I forced myself back into the classroom, even though I was too sick to be there. That action on my part probably made my condition worse. Even after I traded the classroom for the bedroom, I would go to sleep at night and command myself to get up in the morning with my health restored.

But no matter how hard I tried, *I could not get what I wanted.* As author and teacher Byron Katie says: "You can argue with the way things are. You'll lose, but only 100% of the time." I kept losing and losing and losing . . . until I finally stopped arguing and acknowledged my life as it was. Just that acknowledgment eased the mental suffering I was experiencing over having lost my career.

Complaints!

Dissatisfaction can be hard to recognize because it's often such an ordinary part of everyday life that we don't see it even when it's staring us in the face. Some years ago, Tony came up with an objective marker that would help people recognize when dissatisfaction is present for them: *complaints.*

I love the idea of a complaint as a concrete marker for dukkha because it highlights how we project our dissatisfaction out onto the world. The world is simply the way it is. When we complain, we think it's about the world out there, as opposed to how we're *responding* to the world. Even if our complaint is justified—"The neighbors should turn their music down after 10 p.m."—it's still a complaint about the way things are and, as such, reflects dissatisfaction with the world and our lives. Of course, just because something is a complaint doesn't mean we can't take action to change it. The purpose of becoming aware of our complaints is to help us recognize the nature of the dissatisfaction that is present.

Tony and I have turned his idea into a friendly *complaint practice.* "It's too cold in here," one of us declares and the other responds:

"Complaint!" "It's too hot in here." Complaint! "You never turn the lights out when you leave a room." Complaint! "There's nothing on TV." Complaint! "Politicians should stop fighting with each other." Complaint!

This friendly teasing immediately helps us recognize that one of us is in the throes of dukkha, as we resist what is nothing more than another everyday mundane unpleasant experience. Returning to my list of what it would take for me not to be dissatisfied, thinking of dukkha as a complaint helps me see that I can no more control the temperature outside than I can a politician's views—I can't even control the thoughts and emotions that arise in my own mind (thus that crankiness I referred to!).

I hope you'll give this complaint practice a try. You can do it on your own or with another person. You'll quickly discover that whether you're complaining about something unpleasant or about how quickly something pleasant disappears, life simply refuses to always be the way you want it to be or the way you think it should be. You can refuse to accept this; it will add dissatisfaction to your life—but only 100 percent of the time.

More Subtle Clues to the Presence of Dukkha

Dissatisfaction can also be hard to recognize because it can be quite subtle, meaning it can be present without rising to the level of a complaint. If I turn my attention inward and watch what goes on in my mind, I often find a low-grade unease or anguish, and sometimes even dread. In my body, I may notice butterflies in my stomach or tension in certain muscles. I may not identify it as dissatisfaction with my life until I realize that I'm nervous about an upcoming doctor's appointment, or I'm dreading a conversation I need to have with a family member about an ongoing problem.

To help me recognize this unease, I keep in mind a metaphor

for dukkha from Chinese Buddhism: a cart with a slightly broken wheel that gives a jolt each time the wheel rolls over the broken spot. Whenever I feel a slight jolt of being a little off-kilter, I stop and acknowledge that dukkha is present. I often call to mind whichever English word captures the particular flavor of the dukkha I'm experiencing: stress, unease, discontent—and, of course, complaint. With practice, we can learn to recognize these subtle mental and physical clues that are alerting us to the presence of dukkha.

The Buddha had good news for us regarding dukkha. He said we can work with our minds to relieve this dissatisfaction with the circumstances of our lives. To understand how to do this, we first have to examine the source of dukkha. This takes us to the next chapter, and the seemingly unquenchable thirst of *tanha*.

4

Want/Don't-Want: The Unquenchable Thirst

*Just as a fire is covered by smoke and a mirror is
obscured by dust, just as the embryo rests deep within
the womb, wisdom is hidden by selfish desire.*

—THE BHAGAVAD GITA

THE FIRST STEP in freeing ourselves from dukkha is understanding what gives rise to it. The Buddha identified its source as *tanha*. As with dukkha, no one English word conveys the many nuances of tanha. It's usually translated as *desire*, and I'll use that word—as well as *wanting*—to refer to it. But it's important to keep in mind that when the Buddha said the source of dukkha is tanha, he was referring to a particular type of desire, not to all desires.

In the language of the Buddha (Pali), there are over twenty words for what, in English, is expressed by one word: *desire*. So in English, when we use that word, we can be referring to a range of desires—from destructive impulses (such as to harm someone physically) to wholesome aspirations (such as to help someone in need or to raise awareness about environmental pollution).

In Pali, *tanha* refers to a self-focused desire that is often experienced or felt as a need over which we have no control. It can be felt physically and mentally. Tanha's literal translation—*thirst*—comes close to capturing the way it feels. We feel driven by it and think that our happiness and peace of mind depend on getting the right thing or on having certain feelings or experiences. I experience tanha as a felt-sense of lack in my life or in the world—as if something is missing or needs to be set right. I feel as if that lack can only be satisfied by getting my way, just as overwhelming thirst can only be quenched by drinking something.

The reason that tanha is the source of suffering and dissatisfaction in our lives is that fulfilling this type of desire doesn't lead to sustained happiness and peace of mind. That's why tanha is the unquenchable thirst. Our desires are ever changing—what we wanted yesterday isn't what we'll necessarily want today. And if we *do* obtain a desired object or experience (for example, our "dream job"), we can't keep that from changing either (the dream job of today can become the nightmare job of tomorrow if we arrive at work to find a different supervisor or a new set of company policies).

Recall that in English, when we use the word *desire*, we can be referring to a range of desires and wants. The desire that characterizes tanha is not the desire of preferences, even strong preferences—like wanting to eat sushi for dinner or wanting to watch a particular television show. To rise to the level of tanha, we must feel that satisfying the desire in question is deeply tied to our ability to be happy and content in life. (Of course, a person *could* feel this way about eating sushi for dinner, but it would be highly out of the ordinary.)

The Buddha described tanha as not getting what you want or getting what you don't want. I refer to it as the mental state of *want/don't-want* that we live in a good part of every day. Here are some examples of *wants/don't-wants* that can easily rise to the level of tanha:

- *Want*—a material thing (a house of our own), a pleasurable sensory experience (another person's touch), praise or recognition (parent of the year, acclaimed author);
- *Don't-want*—an irritating coworker, a feeling of loneliness, health difficulties.

We're in the realm of tanha when satisfying the above *wants/don't-wants* is more than a preference. Satisfying them feels necessary to our very happiness and peace of mind.

An "If Only" Test for Tanha

One way to recognize the presence of tanha is to notice if we're telling ourselves that we'd be happy and content from then on if only we could fulfill a particular desire. When I was a teenager, I believed that if only I could find the right color of lipstick, I'd be pretty, and if only I were pretty, I'd be happy. In secret, I filled a drawer with dozens of shades I'd bought. With each purchase, I thought, "This is the one what will make me pretty." But soon I'd be dissatisfied and would be searching for another color. I wasn't able to see that my suffering resulted from a sense of lack in my life that had nothing to do with any particular shade of lipstick. I was caught up in a relentless desire to *feel* a certain way—pretty—a desire that I could not satisfy. My heart goes out to my teenage self who thought happiness could be purchased in the form of a shade of lipstick.

And so a good way to distinguish the thirst of tanha from other types of desire is to reflect on whether we've come to regard our happiness and well-being as dependent on satisfying the desire in question. Do we think that if only we could get what we want or get rid of what we don't want, our lives would be dukkha-free? Here are four examples I'll use throughout this chapter:

- If only I could get a promotion, I'd be satisfied;
- If only my kids appreciated all that I do for them, I'd be content with my life;
- If only I didn't feel lonely, I'd be free of problems;
- If only I weren't sick, I'd be happy from now on.

Looking over this list, it's hard to escape the conclusion: Who are we kidding? If all these "if onlys" came to pass, we'd soon realize they didn't bring lasting satisfaction. If we got a promotion, we'd soon want another one, or we'd discover that the new position came with unexpected difficulties. Having appreciative kids would certainly be lovely but wouldn't, in itself, bring permanent happiness and peace of mind. Not feeling lonely wouldn't make for a problem-free life. And, although it would be a relief not to be sick, good health does not "cure" suffering and dissatisfaction.

Tanha keeps us in an underlying perpetual state of wanting, where we think if we can only get the right things or have the right feelings or experiences, we'll find sustained happiness. But the happiness that comes from satisfying this type of desire is short-lived because, as we've learned, everything is impermanent. And so our happiness quickly gives way to new *wants/don't-wants*, leaving us back where we started—with that unquenchable thirst, accompanied by suffering. As adman Don Draper cynically remarked on television's *Mad Men*, "What is happiness? It's a moment before you need more happiness."

The Mind Is Soft and Pliant; Change Is Possible

If it appears that I've painted a bleak picture of the way the mind works, don't worry . . . we can change. The Buddha said this about the mind:

> Just as, of all trees, the balsam is the most soft and pliant, in the same way, I don't envision a single thing that, when developed and cultivated, is as soft and pliant as the mind.

This means that we can transform our mental habits. This involves changing the way we respond when desire arises so that we can free ourselves from being driven by it. There is a profound happiness that's not dependent on getting what we want or getting rid of what we don't want. This happiness is not Don Draper's "a moment before we need more happiness." It's the contented happiness of awakening, a happiness that arises when we're able to live each moment fully as it is without needing it to be different.

Let's examine how we can become more acutely aware of desire and then look at how to work skillfully with it.

Separating Desire from the Object of Desire

Tanha is often present without our even realizing it. This is because we tend to focus on the *object of our desire* instead of on the presence of desire in our own minds and bodies. To illustrate this point, the Thai Buddhist monk Ajahn Jumnian uses the metaphor of the moth and the flame. The moth sees only the flame. Everything else is dark. Seeing only the flame, the moth isn't aware of its own compulsion to fly into it, even though the consequences are fatal.

In the same way, we tend to see only the object of our desire and, as a result, fly into many flames without considering the consequences. The consequences may not be fatal, but they can be the source of much suffering and dissatisfaction. For example, consider the desire to own a house. We can get so caught up in our fantasies about it—the garden we'll plant, the dinner parties we'll host, the identity and status of "home owner" that it will confer—that we don't recognize the intense desire that has arisen in our own minds.

This desire will become the source of suffering and dissatisfaction if we believe that our happiness and contentment are dependent on owning that house. For one thing, having bought it, soon our wanting minds will become focused—like the moth on the flame—on related objects of desire, such as a remodeled kitchen, all new furnishings . . . and, eventually, a bigger house.

Of course, there's nothing wrong with buying and enjoying a house. But we can prevent the suffering and dissatisfaction of dukkha from arising if we understand that being enamored with the object of our desire—the house—may be keeping us from seeing the presence of desire in our own minds. Not only can the failure to see this desire lead to unskillful action (buying a house that we can't afford), it can also delude us into thinking that getting that house is the path to peace and well being.

Working Skillfully with Desire

I've devised a four-step approach for working with desire:

- ▸ Recognize it;
- ▸ Label it;
- ▸ Investigate it;
- ▸ Let it be.

I'll be using these four steps throughout the book to work with a range of stressful and painful mental states. Let's start with the first step: *recognize it*.

As we've seen, recognizing that desire is present in our experience takes practice. But we already have three clues. We can look for the presence of that sense of lack—the feeling that something is wrong and that it can only be set right if we can get our way. Second, we can listen for that voice that says "if only" we could get what we want or get rid of what we don't want, we'd be happy and content. Third, we saw in Ajahn Jumnian's moth-to-flame metaphor that when we find ourselves focused on an object or an experience and begin to feel that we *need* to have it, it's a sign that tanha is present.

Having recognized that desire has arisen, step two is to *label it*. With a silent or soft gentle voice, give it a name. Returning to my four examples, here are some labeling phrases:

- "Desiring a promotion";
- "Wanting my kids to appreciate me";
- "Not wanting to feel lonely";
- "Needing to be healthy again."

The purpose of labeling is to help us hold the desire itself in our conscious awareness, without succumbing to the tendency to turn away from it in aversion or to focus on the object of the desire instead.

Holding the desire in our awareness gives us an opportunity to *investigate it*—the third step in working skillfully with it. The Buddha said that investigation is one of the mental skills that's essential to cultivate on the path of awakening. With desire, we're carefully examining how it operates in our lives. Just learning about it can weaken its hold on us.

As you investigate a particular desire, I urge you not to blame yourself for its presence. Desires arise uninvited in everyone's mind! Our task is to learn how to respond skillfully to them. Maintaining a nonjudgmental attitude helps because we're coaxing desire into the light of mindful awareness. The last thing we want to do is scare it back into the dark recesses of the mind by being critical of ourselves over its presence. If it disappears behind judgment and aversion, it's likely to only grow stronger. So investigate by engaging the desire with nonjudgmental curiosity.

When I investigate a desire, the first thing I notice is that, although it feels as if the suffering is coming from the object of my desire, it's not. It's coming from my own mind. Using my four examples to illustrate this further, we might think it's our situation at work, or our kids' attitude, or the feeling of loneliness, or an illness that's causing us to suffer. But if we investigate, we'll see that the suffering is not coming from these objects of our desire. It's coming from our own wanting or not-wanting minds. We tell ourselves that if we could only get what we want or get rid of what we don't want, we'd find lasting happiness and satisfaction. That's the delusion that most of us live with every day.

Investigating a particular desire might also reveal that certain factors in our environment affect it. It may arise as a result of some *should* or *shouldn't* that we've conjured up for ourselves. It may intensify at certain times of day. It may be harder to refrain from acting on the desire when we're alone. These clues help us to become mindful, objective observers of our desires and this, in turn, makes it easier for us to avoid impulsively acting on them.

One of the most revealing insights into desire that comes from investigation is the realization that we spin stressful and distorted stories about our *wants/don't-wants*. My mind is quite adept at creating a running commentary, which only serves to intensify my suffering. Again, using my four examples, these stories might sound like this:

- ► "I'm not getting a promotion because I'm incompetent";
- ► "My kids don't care about me";
- ► "I'll be lonely the rest of my life";
- ► "I'm ruining my family's life because of my health problems."

Do you see a common thread in these stories? All of them suggest that we're thinking of ourselves as deficient or unworthy in some way.

In 1990, Buddhist teacher Sharon Salzberg attended a conference with the Dalai Lama that was held for Westerners. When it was her turn to bring up an issue for discussion, she asked him, "What do you think about self-hatred?" She was hoping for advice in helping her many students whose inner critic was so strong. The Dalai Lama was utterly confused by her question because he wasn't familiar with the idea of people disliking themselves. It simply wasn't part of his culture.

This story is comforting because it means that we are not inherently deficient or unworthy. These types of feelings are the result of conditioning. And there's no better way to begin "reconditioning" a self-critical mind than to question the validity of the stressful stories it spins. This is one of the most fruitful outcomes of investigation. If we ask ourselves, "Am I sure this thought is true?" we'll realize that we've been feeding the desire in question with a story that may reflect our fears and the feeling that we're not good enough but is unlikely to be true. Might the inability to get a promotion have to do with the company's finances instead of our level of competence? Couldn't our kids care deeply about us but just not express it outwardly? Do we know for sure that we'll be lonely the rest of our lives? Have we asked our loved ones if we're ruining their lives?

As Buddhist teachers sometimes say, the suffering is in the stories. When we understand that these stories reflect our conditioning and are distortions of the past or present, or are worst-case scenarios about a future we can't possibly know, then we can suspend our belief in their validity. That, in itself, can relieve our suffering tremendously.

Those are the first three steps in working skillfully with desire: recognize it, label it, and investigate it. This is how we can come to know our minds.

The final step in working with desire is to *let it be.* Resisting the presence of desire (or any stressful mental state) by commanding ourselves to let go of it may not only strengthen it but is likely to lead to self-blame if we're unsuccessful in our efforts. Every week, I get emails from people berating themselves because they've been told to "let go, let go, let go" but are unable to do so. Rather than trying to force a desire out of our minds with yet another desire— the desire to be rid of the desire—I suggest the more compassionate *let it be.*

Simply be aware of the presence of the desire in question, acknowledging that not all desires can be satisfied, and allowing compassion to arise for whatever suffering the desire is causing. Having shined the light of mindful investigation on the desire may already have loosened its grip, making it easier to patiently wait until it weakens and passes out of the mind.

Like all thoughts and emotions, desire is subject to the law of impermanence and no-fixed-self, so it's not a permanent part of who we are. What a relief to know that we need not identify with a desire as *mine* or as a quality of *me* or *myself.* Even if similar desires return again and again, we know with our wisdom mind that each will pass away, again and again, over and over. Understanding impermanence makes it easier to patiently wait a desire out. The alternatives are to try and force ourselves to let go of it (which may lead to self-blame) or to impulsively act based on it (which may lead to harm to ourselves and others).

Letting a mental state be—even a stressful one—is itself a moment of waking up because, instead of resisting what's present in the moment, we're engaging our experience, as it is, even if it's unpleasant. It's the nature of the mind to give rise to thoughts and emotions, and so by simply letting them be, it's as if we're saying: "It's okay. This is just what's present in this moment. I can be at ease with whatever is arising in the mind."

It takes practice to learn to work skillfully with desire. Most of us will be undoing a lifetime of conditioning in which tanha has driven our behavior. So don't be discouraged if, when you try this four-step approach, you sometimes get lost or it feels like a muddle to you. Just take a deep breath and try again another time. Be patient. The Buddha considered patience to be one of the mental states that an awakened person has perfected (it's one of the "perfections of a Buddha"). To me, patience is an act of compassion toward ourselves, and I hope you'll undertake this four-step approach in that spirit.

After working with desire in this way for a while, sometimes a little miracle happens. We've become so familiar with the mind's tendency to *want/don't-want* that we're able to catch a self-focused desire when it first arises and can choose not to take it up. Then we don't need to label or investigate it because, having become experts at how our own mind works, we're able to just observe the desire when it arises and say, without aversion, "No thank you."

Tanha is the source of suffering and dissatisfaction in our lives, not only because satisfying a desire doesn't bring lasting happiness and peace of mind, but also because living in a constant state of *want/don't-want* reflects discontent with our life as it is. And so, every day, I work on becoming aware of the suffering and dissatisfaction that arise when I'm being driven by desire. In those moments when I can clearly see this, I'm able to refrain from acting on the impulse to try and make the world and my life conform to the way I think they should be.

The difficulties we face in life can help us along the path of awakening because they motivate us to look deeply at tanha. When we do this, we'll see that true peace and well-being are not dependent on getting our way.

5

Looking More Deeply at Suffering and Dissatisfaction

I know but one freedom and that is the freedom of the mind.
—ANTOINE DE SAINT-EXUPÉRY

WE'VE SEEN THAT one of the crucial steps in relieving dukkha is to bring it to conscious awareness. To do this, it helps to understand the different ways we experience suffering and dissatisfaction in our lives. The Buddha described three types of dukkha. They are the subjects of this chapter, along with how we can work on freeing our minds from them.

Aversion to Unpleasant Experiences

The first type of dukkha arises when we react with aversion to life's unpleasant physical or mental experiences. I call this *aversion dukkha*. It arises when, instead of acknowledging that unpleasant experiences—those 10,000 sorrows—are an integral part of everyday life, we tense up and resist the way things are happening.

Unpleasant experiences are felt in both the body and the mind. In 2008, I broke my ankle. There was no way around it—my life at that time included unpleasant physical sensations. In 1995, I lost my best friend Anne to cancer. My mind was overcome with sadness and grief—there was nothing I could do to prevent deep sorrow from arising.

Deep sorrow is not limited to separation by death; it could be separation due to a loved one being deployed overseas or to a relationship dissolving. It could also be due to a child moving out of the house for the first time. (As Tony was driving us home after dropping our son off at college, my sobbing became so intense that he had to pull off the freeway; I think he was afraid I was going to grab the wheel and turn the car around.)

These physical and mental experiences are part of life's ten thousand sorrows. However, it's not the mere presence of these unpleasant experiences that leads to aversion dukkha. It arises from our aversive reaction to them. Aversion dukkha is the *don't-want* side of *want/don't-want*. And so its origin is none other than the self-focused desire that characterizes tanha. We don't want unpleasantness in our lives. Indeed, we often feel as if we have no choice—our very happiness depends on getting rid of it! But the continuous pursuit of *don't-want* desire is like hitting our heads against a wall because we're not going to get our way with any consistency. We were born, and so we are subject to injury, illness, aging, separation, and loss. So are our loved ones. Life can be very tough at times.

The good news is that we need not add the suffering of aversion dukkha to the mix. The way to prevent it from arising is to change our response to unpleasant experiences by acknowledging them as unpleasant but not rejecting them with that *don't-want* mentality. Then, knowing with our wisdom mind that everything is impermanent, we can just be with the unpleasantness until it runs its course.

Not surprisingly, this is easier said than done. It requires mindfulness and effort. When I was consciously aware of the physical pain—"This broken ankle hurts"—and of the emotional pain—"This grief from Anne's death is hard to bear"—but didn't resist the unpleasantness, aversion dukkha did not arise. The physical pain from my broken ankle ran its course. Eventually, the grief over the loss of my friend transformed into fond memories.

Perhaps the Tibetan Buddhist teacher Pema Chödrön was referring to aversion dukkha when she said, "Hell is just resistance to life."

Desiring Pleasant Experiences to Be Permanent

Whereas aversion dukkha arises in response to unpleasant experiences, this type of dukkha arises in response to pleasant ones. When we're enjoying a pleasant experience, we want it to continue. In fact, we'll go to extremes to keep it going (staying out too late, drinking too much). And so, as with aversion dukkha, this dukkha has its origin in the desire and wanting of tanha. We want our pleasant experiences to be permanent, even though, if we reflect on it, we know that's not possible. I call this type of dukkha *impermanence dukkha.*

Impermanence dukkha can arise in the midst of a pleasant experience, interfering with our ability to enjoy it. Our joy is tainted by the underlying dissatisfaction of knowing, at a gut level, that the experience won't last. Have you ever felt unease in the midst of having a great time, perhaps while you were at a concert or spending time with someone special? I remember sitting outside in the evening on the island of Moloka'i, watching a spectacular orange and red sunset with palm trees silhouetted in the foreground. I wondered why this joyful experience contained an underlying discontent. Now I know. The desire for it to last forever was gnawing at me. That's impermanence dukkha.

As Richard Gombrich points out in *What the Buddha Thought*, nothing that is impermanent can be fully satisfactory:

> The Buddha saw that normal experience is vitiated by the transience of all worldly phenomena, a transience which must sooner or later render them unsatisfying. Our experience of their transience can only successfully be handled, he argued, by coming to terms with it: we should not want permanence, for ourselves or our loved ones, because we are not going to get it.

This illustrates how desire underlies this type of dukkha—desire for the impermanent to be permanent. But as the Buddha pointed out, and as we can confirm for ourselves, we're not going to get it. And so it is for everyone.

Spinning Stressful Stories

A third type of dukkha arises when we concoct stressful stories about the bare facts of our experience and then talk ourselves into believing that these stories reflect the way things are. As mentioned in the previous chapter, the suffering is in the stories, stories that often reveal how we've been conditioned to be our own harshest critics—that Western tendency that so baffled the Dalai Lama.

I call this type of dukkha *storytelling dukkha*. These stories take three forms: ruminating with regret over the past, engaging in a running commentary about what's going on right now, and concocting worst-case scenarios about the future. Like aversion dukkha and impermanence dukkha, storytelling dukkha has its origin in tanha, because this stressful thinking reflects the desire for our lives to have turned out a particular way in the past, to be a particular way now, or to avoid a particular course in the future.

Storytelling dukkha often arises on the heels of the other two types of dukkha, compounding the suffering we're already enduring. To illustrate this, I'll revisit three examples I've been using. I broke my ankle and it hurt. When I was able to simply be with the pain and its unpleasantness, aversion dukkha did not arise. It arose when I resisted the presence of pain; then storytelling dukkha was not far behind in the form of stressful thoughts. I ruminated about the past: "It's my fault that I fell; how could I be so clumsy?" I added stressful commentary to the bare experience of the physical pain: "It's not fair that I broke my ankle when I'm already sick." And I mocked up worst-case scenarios about the future: "What if it doesn't heal correctly?"

A second example. When Anne died, aversion dukkha arose in those moments when I turned away from the sorrow in aversion. Then, when I added stressful thoughts, such as "I should be over this grief already" and even "I should *never* get over this grief," I was in the throes of storytelling dukkha. (Somehow the fact that I'd managed to conjure two contradictory scenarios regarding the circumstances of my life and found both to be unsatisfactory did not, at the time, strike me as the least bit remarkable!)

And finally, as I watched that Moloka'i sunset, impermanence dukkha arose in the form of unease and discontent because I wanted it to last all night even though I knew it couldn't. This spoiled my ability to simply enjoy the unfolding display of colors. Then, compounding my suffering, storytelling dukkha arose. I started by adding distracting commentary to what was happening in the moment: "How much longer will it look like this? Ten minutes?

Five minutes? Two minutes?" Then I topped it off with a stressful story about the future: "Maybe tomorrow night, after we've left the island, it will be even more spectacular and we'll miss out on it."

We can't control the thoughts and stories that pop into our minds, but we can learn to respond to them skillfully. On a retreat, Buddhist teacher Ayya Khema told us at one point that thoughts arise like the air around us and are arbitrary and unreliable. Then she looked at us intensely and said in her stern German accent: "Most of them are just rubbish, but we believe them anyway." Until she said this, it had never occurred to me to question the validity of my stressful thoughts. I had never understood that I didn't have to believe those thoughts just because they arose.

Mindfulness and investigation can help us learn to respond skillfully to our stressful thoughts and stories. We can start by asking, "What am I telling myself about this situation that's making me feel worse?" This brings our stories into conscious awareness so we can begin to examine the assumptions that underlie them.

These assumptions often involve our clinging to an idea of how we think things *should* be, which just sets us up for suffering. Was it true that breaking an ankle when I was already sick wasn't fair? (The fact is, injury and illness are not mutually exclusive.) Was it true that I shouldn't feel so much grief over Anne's death . . . or that I should never stop grieving lest I forget her? (Neither assertion is constructive.) Learning to question the credibility of the stories we spin can help free us from the negative self-judgment and the suffering they give rise to.

Mindfulness and investigation also make us acutely aware of the impermanent nature of our thoughts. This helps relieve storytelling dukkha because, even if stressful thoughts persist after we've questioned their validity, we know they're not permanently lodged in our minds. I like to think of thoughts as fluid events, floating through the mind. This helps me hold them more lightly.

We can also relieve storytelling dukkha by cultivating the open-hearted states of mind referred to in Chapter Three, such as compassion and equanimity. Evoking these for ourselves is a powerful antidote to stressful thinking. With my broken ankle, compassion took the form of gently saying to myself, "My poor broken ankle—hurting, hurting, hurting." With the loss of my dear friend, equanimity took the form of softly repeating, "Grieving is painful but this is what my life is about right now."

The Tracing Exercise

Becoming familiar with the three types of dukkha and the self-focused desire that gives rise to each of them opens the door to relieving our suffering and dissatisfaction. To review the three types: resisting unpleasant experiences leads to aversion dukkha; wanting pleasant experiences to last gives rise to impermanence dukkha; and spinning stressful stories about our lives—stories we then come to believe without question—puts us squarely in the realm of storytelling dukkha.

I've devised a practice I call *the tracing exercise* to help me identify the desire that's at the source of any dukkha I might be experiencing. I start by paying attention to when suffering or dissatisfaction are present in my experience. This itself can be a challenge because, as noted in Chapter Three, dukkha can be subtle and hard to recognize. It helps to recall the many words used to describe it, such as stress or discomfort—even unhappiness. It also helps to look for *complaints* or for that off-kilter feeling of unease from that Chinese metaphor for dukkha of a cart with a slightly broken wheel.

Once I identify that dukkha is present, I keep it steady in my mind. Then I begin to trace my experience backward until I'm able to identify the desire that characterizes tanha—the place where getting what I want or getting rid of what I don't want feels necessary to my happiness and well-being. Having traced the dukkha to the presence of this desire, I use the four-step approach from the previous chapter:

- ▸ Recognize it;
- ▸ Label it;
- ▸ Investigate it;
- ▸ Let it be.

This tracing exercise, coupled with the four-step approach, is an effective way to ease the pain of dukkha.

Here's how I could have used this technique to relieve impermanence dukkha when I was watching the Moloka'i sunset. First, I'd become aware of how, in the midst of this joyful experience, I'm feeling off kilter—that there's dissatisfaction and discontent gnawing at the edges of the beautiful view. I'd trace that feeling backward until I recognized its origin. And there it would be—in my desire for that sunset to last for hours.

I'd use labeling to keep the desire steady in my awareness— "wanting this sunset to last for hours." Then I'd investigate it. I'd feel the tension it's creating in my mind and body. I'd reflect on how I could cling to this desire as long as I wanted, but it wouldn't affect the fleeting nature of the sunset. This is simply one of those circumstances in life that I have no power to control. Then, bowing with my wisdom mind to the law of impermanence, I'd enjoy the pleasant experience while it lasts, without dissatisfied longing creeping in to pollute the simplicity of the joy. Had I used this technique on that Moloka'i evening, watching the sunset would have been a moment of awakening because I'd have been engaging my experience just as it was, without clinging to it. This is an example of navigating joy skillfully.

Here's how I've used the tracing exercise and the four-step approach to relieve aversion dukkha and storytelling dukkha.

During the 2010 holiday season, I was home by myself (as I often am) and began to feel uncharacteristically cranky and irritable. It took me by surprise because I've come to enjoy solitude. But there I was, off kilter. Instead of letting it brew until it turned into a full-blown bout of suffering and misery, I began the tracing exercise.

Soon I recognized the source of my irritable mood. I wanted to be with my family and was immensely sad that I couldn't be. However, instead of acknowledging the presence of this unpleasant emotion, I was resisting it; I wanted to get rid of it. In short, I didn't want to be feeling what I was feeling. That resistance was aversion dukkha. Then I added to the resistance a host of stressful stories about how I thought things *should* be—stories I believed without question. "I should be able to travel even though I'm sick." "I'm a weak person because I can't handle being alone." There I was, in the throes of aversion dukkha and storytelling dukkha because I could not get my way—I wanted to be with my family and I didn't want to feel sad about not being with them!

Investigating aversion dukkha and storytelling dukkha in this fashion loosened their hold on me, especially when I realized the utter foolishness of those stories I was spinning. I also knew that trying to push my sadness away in aversion would only strengthen it, so I let it be. Just calling to mind those words, "let it be," eased my irritation.

Then, wrapping myself in a cloak of compassion over my sadness, I found something soothing to do and patiently waited until those *want/don't-want* desires wore themselves out and passed out of my mind. When they finally did, I felt at peace with my circumstances. It was the peace of mind that arises when we're able to navigate sorrow skillfully.

Learning to recognize dukkha in its various forms, using the tracing exercise to identify the desire that is its source, and then employing the four-step approach can give us welcome respite from being mindlessly driven to try and fashion every circumstance of our lives to be to our liking. It also offers that taste of "freedom of the mind" that Antoine de Saint-Exupéry refers to in the quotation that begins this chapter. It's a taste that can inspire us to keep practicing.

6

Five Habits of Mind that Are
Obstacles to Waking Up

Fear is a habit. I am not afraid.

—AUNG SAN SUU KYI

THE BUDDHA IDENTIFIED five habits of mind that are obstacles on the path of awakening because they hinder or
cloud our ability to see clearly the three marks of experience—
impermanence, no-fixed-self, and dukkha. Called the *five hindrances* in Buddhism, they are collectively known by other
names—demons, negative energies, temptations—in almost all
spiritual and religious traditions.

All five hindrances are familiar to us, but each of us seems to
have our own "areas of specialization," meaning that, as a result of
our past conditioning and our unique life experiences, some of the
hindrances have become more individually entrenched as mental
habits than others. We'll look at each of the five in turn and then
practice working with them.

Desire for Sense Pleasure

There's nothing wrong with having a good time, but when we're caught up in this hindrance, we actively, sometimes obsessively, pursue pleasurable experiences through our sense doors. In Buddhist thought, the mind is considered to be the sixth sense, so the sense doors would be: sight, sound, smell, taste, bodily sensations, and thoughts and emotions. This hindrance takes the form of desiring to please those senses to the exclusion of other experiences. We want to hear our favorite music, eat our favorite foods, experience pleasurable body sensations, have only pleasant thoughts and emotions.

The desire for sense pleasure lacks the compulsive quality of tanha—that seemingly unquenchable thirst that we've been examining in previous chapters. Tanha is experienced as that "if only" *need*—we think our happiness depends on satisfying the desire in question. In contrast, the hindrance, desire for sense pleasure, is experienced as a strong preference for experiences that please us. We'd *like* that chocolate brownie because we love sweets, but we're not thinking, "If only I could eat it, I'd be at peace with my life." We'd *like* the movie we're watching to have a happy ending, but we don't think we *need* it to end happily in order to be happy ourselves.

Desire for sense pleasure becomes an obstacle to awakening when it leads us to continually chase after pleasant experiences. We can easily come to desire and even expect that everything we encounter will please us. This clouds our ability to see that life is an ever-changing mixture of pleasant and unpleasant experiences—joys and sorrows. And so we're setting ourselves up for suffering when we continually pursue pleasant experiences, because an unending parade of pleasantness is not possible.

True happiness is an inner peace not dependent on all of our experiences being pleasurable.

Anger or Ill-Will

When we're caught up in this hindrance, we're quick to criticize and judge. Nothing meets the standards we set up and then cling to as "right." No wonder we're unhappy! Anger or ill-will can range in intensity from mild irritation, to resentment, to destructive outbursts of rage. We may criticize others: "She doesn't know what she's talking about"; "He's full of crap." We may criticize ourselves. I used to be angry at myself for not recovering my health. The anger took the form of self-blame and recrimination. It added an extra layer of misery to the symptoms of the illness. It took me years to realize that this anger was just a way to keep me from experiencing the deep sorrow I was feeling.

When our wisdom mind is clouded by this hindrance, we don't see that life's mixture of joys and difficulties, successes and disappointments applies to us too, and so we get angry when circumstances and other people don't conform to our liking. But anger gives rise to suffering. The Buddha said that when we direct anger at another, it comes right back to us—like fine dust thrown against the wind. In my experience, when I direct anger at myself, it also comes right back at me, in the form of suffering.

Torpor or Lethargy

This hindrance doesn't refer to bodies that are sick or in pain or simply need to rest; the hindrances are mental states. This one is characterized by apathy and lethargy—a feeling of staleness and lack of enthusiasm in the mind. Everything is too much effort, as in, "I can't be bothered," or "This is too much of a hassle." If you've raised teenagers, you've experienced this hindrance in action. If you ask them to clean their room, they'll say, "I don't have the energy." If you then say, "Okay, then you must not have the energy to go for an ice cream," they'll perk right up and say, "Sure I do," and this hindrance will disappear from their minds!

More seriously, torpor and lethargy can take hold of us at a deep level. The lack of enthusiasm in the mind can permeate our whole day. We can't be bothered to keep an engagement. It's too much trouble to fix a meal. We couldn't care less about life. This hindrance is a painful obstacle to awakening because we don't have the energy to engage life.

Restlessness or Worry

When this hindrance arises, we're anxious, agitated, and often fearful. Both restlessness and worry stem from an uneasiness about life. Restlessness reflects an uneasiness about the present, and worry reflects an uneasiness about the future. When we're restless, we have difficulty being still in the moment. We want to be moving all the time—do this, do that, do *anything* but be still because something better than whatever is present must be right around the corner.

When we're worrying, we're afraid that things are going to go wrong. We think that if we could only anticipate what's going to happen in the future, we could prepare for it. As a result, we obsess over every imaginable possibility. I know, because this is my particular area of specialization, and storytelling dukkha is its primary feature: "If I'm in an accident and taken to the hospital, will they understand that I'm already chronically ill?" "What if Tony gets sick or injured and suddenly needs *me* to be the caregiver?" These worst-case scenarios are a great source of suffering for me—unnecessary suffering since it's impossible to predict the future.

The words *worry* and *fear* are often used interchangeably and I'll be doing so here. Fear *can* arise without worry—and be constructive—such as when an immediate danger triggers fear that results in a fight-or-flight response. But worry and fear usually go hand in hand.

They can arise over mundane matters—"If this traffic doesn't start moving, I'm afraid I'll be late for lunch." Or they can arise over profound concerns—"If my parents' health deteriorates and they can't live independently, who will take care of them?" Both worry and fear focus our attention on some imagined event or experience in the future. Of course, skillful planning for the future is a wise use of our time and can prevent much suffering in the years to come. But there's a difference between thoughtful planning and persistent worrying about the future. The latter is the hindrance that we'll be working with.

Both restlessness and worry cloud our ability to wake up to the moment because they keep us from being at peace with our life as it is right now. When we're restless, we're always thinking something better must be around the corner. When we're worrying, we're too lost in fearful thoughts about the future to be able to embrace the present moment.

Skeptical Doubt

There is skillful doubt—not believing something just because we've heard it somewhere else, but instead seeking to verify it ourselves— and there is skeptical doubt. Skeptical doubt is characterized by the constant wavering between belief and disbelief.

With skeptical doubt, we find ourselves skipping from this belief to that one and from one spiritual practice to another when, in fact, any number of paths might be to our benefit. I once had myself enrolled in three overlapping meditation retreats—one Zen, one Tibetan, and one Theravadin—because I couldn't decide which one held the magic key to the peace and well-being I was seeking. This served only to increase my suffering as I directed negative self-judgment at myself: "You can never settle on anything!"

When our wisdom mind is clouded by this hindrance, we can't see clearly that this relentless questioning of our assessments and decisions is keeping us from embracing wholeheartedly what we're doing, right now, in this moment.

Working Skillfully with the Hindrances

As if we don't have our work cut out for us when only one hindrance arises, it's very common for one hindrance to arise on the heels of another. Buddhist teachers often lightheartedly refer to this as a *multiple hindrance attack*. The usual culprit is the second hindrance, anger. It shows up as aversion to the presence of whichever hindrance has arisen.

The aversion takes these forms: "I hate this desire"; "I don't want to feel this lethargy"; "Worry is ruining my day." And because aversion usually carries a negative judgment about ourselves along with it—"I shouldn't feel this way"—the result is suffering in abundance. I'm quite sure none of you are strangers to feeling aversion to these five habits of mind.

Learning to respond skillfully to the hindrances minimizes their impact on our lives. For most of us, each of the hindrances will arise from time to time. When they do, how we respond to them will affect the depth of suffering that results.

To work skillfully with the hindrances, we'll use the four-step approach from the last two chapters, except we'll apply it to the hindrances instead of to the type of desire that characterizes tanha. I'll go through the four steps and then we'll practice with several of the hindrances.

The first step is to *recognize it*—become aware that a hindrance has arisen. This can be a challenge because our attention can become

so focused on the *object* of the hindrance—the chocolate brownie, the person we're angry at, the appointment we're worried about, the spiritual practice we're doubting—that we don't even recognize that we're in the throes of the hindrance itself. Good mindfulness skills can help here. With practice and patience, we can become adept at recognizing that a hindrance is present in the mind.

Having recognized the presence of the hindrance, *label it*. Giving it a name helps us hold it as an object of our awareness so that we can investigate it. In the written record of the Buddha's teaching, he often used the words "I see you" to label the various mental states that were obstacles to awakening. When I imagine the Buddha speaking this phrase, I hear him saying it in a friendly tone, not a frustrated or hostile one. This is because I've discovered that a friendly tone keeps aversion to the hindrance from arising or, if it's already arisen, keeps it from intensifying. I call this attitude of friendliness toward the hindrances *treating the hindrances as guests*.

I started treating them as guests when I realized how often I was adding to the simple presence of a hindrance, thoughts about how much I disliked it, followed by a negative self-judgment for feeling this dislike. Call it suffering upon suffering upon suffering. How we can make ourselves miserable over a simple arising and passing event in the mind!

So try treating the hindrance as a guest, even if it doesn't feel genuine at first. If you like, you can say something like the Buddha did: "I see you." Being friendly has the most disarming effect on the hindrance in question. It stops aversion to it from arising or, if aversion has already arisen, it steals its thunder. We're friendly to our guests when they show up unexpectedly. Well, when we're friendly to the hindrances, aversion to them never gets a foothold.

Because we've labeled the hindrance in a friendly manner, we can *investigate it* (step 3) without aversion. Start by noticing how the hindrance feels in the body. Pleasant? Unpleasant? Are there areas

of tension or discomfort? Just as our physical condition can affect our thoughts and emotions, what's going on in the mind can affect the body. The mind and the body are interconnected, so noticing the bodily sensations that accompany a hindrance increases our overall awareness of it.

Then we can begin to investigate how the presence of the hindrance makes us feel mentally. Does it feel pleasant? Unpleasant? Once again, mindfulness is an important tool: it's one thing to be aware that we're angry; it's quite another to be aware of how that anger makes us feel.

We can check to see if we're treating the hindrance as a fixed part of who we are—"angry person," "worrywart," "always indecisive." Identifying with it as a fixed self inclines the mind toward the hindrance in question, and this creates the causes and conditions for it to become a repeating pattern in the mind. It also feeds any feelings of unworthiness—that inner critic that so many of us carry around. So instead of identifying with the hindrance, try treating it as an arising and passing event in the mind.

We can also look for the *want/don't-want* of tanha that's behind the hindrance. In other words, what is it that we want but aren't getting? What is it that we're getting that we don't want? It's also fruitful to examine any stories we're telling ourselves in relation to the hindrance. Are we spinning exaggerated tales and worst-case scenarios and then believing them without question? This is storytelling dukkha. If it's helpful, recall Ayya Khema's assessment of thoughts: most of them are just rubbish, but we believe them anyway.

This investigation holds the promise for transforming these deeply ingrained habits of mind. For example, we may know from the law of impermanence that if restlessness arises, it will eventually pass out of the mind. But unless we investigate the restlessness—how it feels physically and mentally, the nature of the desire that's

behind it, whether we're identifying with it as a fixed self, the stories we tell ourselves about it—it's likely to pop right back into the mind again. With mindful investigation, we're gradually coming to know our own mind—what makes us tick! And the better we know our mind, the better able we are to incline it toward kind and nonharmful thoughts, speech, and actions.

Finally, having investigated the hindrance as best we can (sometimes we'll be more successful than other times), we just *let it be*. Recoiling from it or trying to force it out of the mind with a "let it go" command may only strengthen it and is likely to lead to self-blame if our efforts fail. Instead, with compassion toward ourselves for any suffering the presence of the hindrance is causing, we patiently let it be, knowing that it will eventually yield to the law of impermanence and pass out of the mind. Letting it be can be a moment of awakening because we're accepting unconditionally—without aversion—that this is how we feel at the present moment.

When working with the hindrances in this way, be content to take baby steps and be ready to lose your way sometimes. If you get lost in the throes of anger or worry or another hindrance and you're not able to go through these four steps, that's fine. Take a deep breath and know that in the next moment, you can start the practice anew. We can go from dukkha to no dukkha—from suffering to no suffering—over and over again! And if you can't concentrate on the four steps at this moment, that's okay too. Wrap yourself in a cloak of compassion, safe in the knowledge that the law of impermanence is on your side and that the hindrance will eventually weaken and pass out of your mind.

Practicing with Desire for Sense Pleasure

Many years ago, I was at a daylong retreat with Buddhist teacher Ruth Denison. Everyone had brought a dish to share for lunch.

When the time came to eat, we lined up at the front of two long tables that were filled with food. Then Ms. Denison took us by surprise. She said, "Before you take a dish and start serving yourselves, everyone is to walk slowly by the tables—twice—and notice your desire for the food." As I walked past the food the first time, if you'd asked me if I was caught up in the desire for sense pleasure, I'd have said "no!"

But as I began to walk past the food the second time, suddenly the sensory pleasure I was experiencing from seeing and smelling the food was overwhelming. I wanted her to call off this silly exercise so that I could get those mouth-watering morsels into my body as soon as possible! I knew I couldn't very well start grabbing at the food. So, not without irritation, I decided to give in to her instructions and simply notice the presence of desire in my mind and body and see if I could feel its pull on me.

Amazingly, recognizing and investigating the desire in this fashion became more interesting to me than the food itself. I noticed that being hungry was a sensation in my body but that wanting to eat was a mental state. It was a thought I could label: "Desire to eat this food." By the time I walked down the line the third time, the desire had subsided. I filled my plate slowly, with a feeling of gratitude toward those who had taken the time to fix such delicious food to share.

I learned so much from Ms. Denison about how desire for sense pleasure works that I've tried her exercise at home. I choose a meal that contains some of my favorite food. Instead of picking up my utensil and diving right in, I stop for three to five minutes and notice everything I can about the food—how it looks, how it smells, how I feel about it. Recognizing that desire for sense pleasure has arisen, I label it: "Wanting this food; "Desire has arisen for this food."

Sometimes I realize that I'm telling myself stories about how I've

learned the lesson of the exercise already: "I get the point—desire for sense pleasure can be powerful—so there's no good reason not to eat right now!" When this happens, I note the thoughts and then let them be, knowing with my wisdom mind that they're just arising and passing events in the mind.

I encourage you to try this. The idea here is not to take a negative view of wanting delicious food but to begin to make the hindrance of desire for sense pleasure a more conscious part of your everyday life. When you do this, you'll begin to recognize how often you chase after sense pleasure and how this can lead you to expect all of your experiences to be pleasant—a surefire set-up for suffering!

Practicing with Anger

When anger arises, we tend to get so caught up in the object of our anger—"How can she get away with that?" or "He's dead wrong"—that our ability to see clearly is hindered. Specifically, we don't realize that it's the anger in our own mind and not the object toward which that anger is directed that's making us suffer.

But we can learn to handle anger skillfully. First, of course, we work on recognizing that it's arisen. Then we label it: "Mind filled with anger"; "I see you, anger." If we label it with a nonjudgmental attitude, as if we're hosting an old friend, we can keep it from intensifying.

Investigating the anger, we can ask ourselves how it feels physically and mentally. Does it tend to arise in the presence of certain people or at certain times of day or when we're too busy or feeling tired? Can we pinpoint the desire behind the anger—what it is that we want that we're not getting, or what it is that we're getting that we don't want? Are we making the anger worse by telling ourselves stories about it? If so, can we dispassionately ask ourselves, "Am I positive this is a true reflection of how things are?"

With increased awareness and a better understanding of how anger works in our minds, we can develop the skill of refraining from speaking or acting out of anger, so that we don't harm ourselves or others. This refraining is how we let the anger be, patiently waiting until it passes out of the mind.

Many years ago when I was in law school, I was in a study group with six other students. One evening, I got into an argument with another student over how to interpret a case that we'd studied in class. He and I disagreed and neither of us was willing to budge. The more we argued, the deeper each of us dug our heels in. "I'm right; you're wrong" is a common story underlying anger.

Now I look back on the incident and realize that I thought I was angry because he refused to acknowledge that I was right and he was wrong. But if I'd had the skills to bring that anger into mindful awareness and investigate it, I would have seen that my anger wasn't due to what he did or didn't believe. It was due to my own self-focused desire—my perceived need—to be right (and the accompanying fear that perhaps I wasn't).

This desire was then compounded by two more desires—to impress the other students in the group and to not be embarrassed in front of them. (He probably felt the same way.) As I kept arguing, I was also silently spinning stories about what I perceived my fellow students to be thinking about me, even though, of course, I had no idea what was going on in their minds. These stories only served to increase the high level of stress I was already feeling. And so the two of us continued with this fruitless argument—fruitless partly because, as it turned out, the interpretation of the case wasn't clear to the professor either! All I got for my time and effort was a lot of suffering.

Because of my Buddhist practice, if this same scene were to play out today, I'm confident that I'd recognize early in the process that what started out as a disagreement over a legal issue had degraded into a battle of one anger-filled mind against another, and that nothing but dukkha was going to come out of it. Once each of us made our points, I'd say something like: "Let's agree to disagree. We can ask the professor about it in class."

Another example. A few years ago, I was referred to a specialist to find out if he had any ideas for treating my mysterious illness. He exuded confidence and told me emphatically that he'd find out what was wrong and then treat me. He ordered a battery of tests. But when the tests came back negative, he was curt and dismissive, simply telling me to go back to my primary care physician.

When I left the follow-up appointment, I was angry. I could feel the anger in my body. My chest was tight, my face was flushed, and I started sweating. Then I began to spin stressful stories that served only to feed the anger: "He had no business making promises he couldn't keep"; "That's the last doctor I'm going to trust." My suffering over this incident lasted for months.

Looking back on it, I see how I could have handled it more skillfully. It's not that I was wrong in thinking that the doctor shouldn't have made those promises. But it wasn't the doctor's behavior that was making me suffer. In other words, my suffering wasn't due to the object of my anger—the doctor. It was due to what was going on in my own mind. Behind the anger that I was directing at him was an intense desire to recover my health. And *that* was the source of my suffering: my inability to get what I wanted.

As for the doctor, yes, he probably shouldn't have acted so assured at that first visit (although maybe he really *did* think he could cure me), and it would have been nice if he'd been more compassionate at the follow-up. But as I like to say about the medical profession: some doctors come through for us and some don't. Just like everything and everyone else in life.

Since this incident, I've had two similar experiences with other doctors, and yes, I was disappointed each time. But I didn't get angry. Now I know that anger only harms me. It doesn't get me better medical care, and it doesn't help me regain my health.

Practicing with Worry and Fear

Now we come to my own special hindrance. As I mentioned, one of my recurring worries is that Tony will get sick or be injured. I conjure up stories where I'd need to be at his bedside in the hospital, navigating the healthcare system and providing him with love and support. These stories trigger worry and fear because, right now, I'm too sick to be able to do this.

If I resist feeling these two painful mental states when they arise, they get more intense. So I work on being mindfully present with them. When I recognize that worry and fear have arisen, I hold them in conscious awareness by gently labeling them with a friendly voice. I use phrases like these: "Worry and fear"; "Worry is present"; "Mind filled with fear." Sometimes I use the Buddha's label: "I see you, worry. I see you, fear."

Maintaining friendliness is important because otherwise I slip into aversion and that invariably carries with it a negative judgment about myself in the form of commentary like, "Can't I stop this constant worrying?" or "I shouldn't feel this way." So I throw aversion off guard by treating worry and fear like old guests.

Then I investigate how they feel. I experience worry and fear as a heaviness, both mentally and physically, as if I'm carrying an extra weight around. When I investigate what gives rise to worry and fear, I find that it's my desire to control the future. That realization loosens their grip because I know with my wisdom mind that controlling the future is impossible. Peace is only to be found by acknowledging the truth of those two corollaries of impermanence: uncertainty and unpredictability. This means there's no more reason for me to assume that Tony will get sick or be injured than there is to assume that he won't. All those stories I spin in which I project *this* medical crisis and *that* medical crisis serve only to increase my stress and suffering.

Fear and worry are habits of mind and habits can change, as Aung San Suu Kyi courageously asserts in the quotation at the beginning of this chapter: "Fear is a habit. I am not afraid." Continually questioning the validity of these stressful scenarios that I spin is one of the ways I'm changing this painful habit.

Working this way with worry and fear weakens them. Then, evoking compassion for myself over the suffering that accompanies these painful mental states, I let them be, knowing that they'll eventually yield to the law of impermanence and pass out of my mind.

It takes time to learn how to respond skillfully to the hindrances, but by practicing in this way, we can gradually transform our responses to these painful and disruptive mental states. The hindrances arise as a result of various causes and conditions in our lives. By maintaining a nonjudgmental attitude toward these habits of mind, we can coax them out of the darkness so that we can shine the light of mindfulness and investigation on them. If we're self-critical or judgmental about their presence, they may retreat back into hiding where they'll only intensify, along with our suffering. So investigate these mental states with curiosity and with patience.

And, as is the case with the *want/don't-want* desire of tanha, we can reach a point where we know our minds well enough that we can catch a hindrance right when it arises and then consciously choose not to take it up. Sometimes just treating the hindrance as a guest is all it takes to stop it in its tracks. And when this happens, we experience the peace of mind that comes with relief from suffering.

Cultivating Mindfulness

7

The Mindfulness Path

Ten thousand flowers in spring,
the moon in autumn,
a cool breeze in summer,
snow in winter.
If your mind isn't clouded by unnecessary things,
this is the best season of your life.
—ZEN MASTER WU-MEN

TAKE THREE OR FOUR conscious breaths, while letting your attention settle on whatever is appearing in your field of awareness—a sight, a sound, a smell, a taste, a bodily sensation, a fleeting thought or emotion or image. There. You've just practiced mindfulness!

Intentionally paying attention to our present-moment experience, without liking it or disliking it, is the essence of mindfulness. The sensation of the breath as it comes in and out of the body is often used as an anchor because the sensations of breathing always exist only in the moment. We can't simultaneously be aware of the sensation of the breath *and* be lost in stories, whether they be about the past, the present, or the future.

Mindfulness is both a tool for cultivating wisdom and a path in itself of awakening. In the first section of the book, we examined how to cultivate wisdom by working on becoming aware of the three marks of experience that the Buddha identified as common to all of us: we're subject to impermanence; we cannot find a fixed, unchanging self; and we'll face suffering and dissatisfaction. We also looked at the five hindrances—those painful habits of mind that are obstacles to waking up because they cloud our ability to see the three marks. Let's begin by considering how mindfulness is an essential tool for cultivating wisdom.

Impermanence and No-Fixed-Self

Intentionally bringing our attention to the present moment helps us recognize the fleeting nature of all our experience—from what we're seeing and hearing to the thoughts and emotions that arise in the mind. We become aware that trying to hold on to pleasant experiences—those ten thousand flowers in Wu-Men's poem—is futile because they will inevitably yield to the law of impermanence. Then with our wisdom mind, we can fully enjoy the experience just as it is, while it lasts.

Mindful awareness of impermanence also helps us realize there's no need to resist unpleasant experiences. The ten thousand sorrows are an inevitable part of life; resisting them intensifies our suffering. Instead, we can be with our experience as it is and wait for the unpleasantness to change.

Cultivating mindfulness, we see that each moment of our lives is different, and every moment holds the possibility of awakening to how things are if we accept and engage the moment as it is, letting go of our desire to fashion every experience to our liking.

When we consciously focus our attention on the present moment, we don't get stuck in self-limiting identities. We become as fluid and changeable as the phenomena around us. One moment we're feeding the dog, the next moment we're talking to a friend on the phone, the next moment we're composing an email. When we give our attention over fully to each of those moments, there's no reason to attach a fixed label to ourselves. We are part of the free flow of the universe. This is living the truth of no-fixed-self.

Suffering and Dissatisfaction

When we're paying attention to the present moment, we're more attuned to the subtleties of our experience. This makes it more likely that we'll recognize dukkha in all its manifestations—stress, unease, anguish, discontent. Sometimes simply becoming mindfully aware that dukkha is present begins to ease our suffering. This awareness also gives us the opportunity to investigate the source of our suffering and dissatisfaction by tracing our experience back to that place where we're either not getting what we want or we're getting what we don't want—the self-focused desire that characterizes tanha.

Mindfulness of desire holds the promise of finding relief from the suffering that comes from the delusion that to be happy, everything has to turn out the way we think it should. Zen Master Dogen succinctly expressed why the desire to control our experience can only lead to suffering: "Nevertheless, flowers fall with our attachment and weeds spring up with our aversion."

When we understand with our wisdom mind that this constant effort to fulfill our desires will not lead to lasting happiness and satisfaction, it's easier not to impulsively act on them. We can let them be and patiently wait for them to change and pass out of the mind on their own. This insight into desire and the suffering it causes is a moment of awakening because, when we're not under the spell of desire, we're present for our experience just as it is—what Zen teachers often call *just this*.

The Hindrances

Mindfulness also enables us to work skillfully with the hindrances—those habits of mind that intensify our suffering by clouding our ability to see the three marks of experience. For example, if the hindrance of anger arises, instead of acting out of anger in a way that might harm ourselves or others, we can start to practice mindfulness of the anger. By keeping the anger present in our awareness, we can investigate it and find the desire behind it and the stories we're telling ourselves that feed the anger. Drawing on these insights, we can then choose not to take it up—not to speak or act upon it but instead let it be, as it changes and eventually passes out of the mind.

With practice, mindfulness holds the promise for us to change these habits of mind that cloud our ability to see clearly and so are obstacles to waking up. As Wu-Men says in the poem that begins this chapter, the best season of our life is when our minds aren't clouded by unnecessary things.

In addition to being a tool for cultivating wisdom, mindfulness is a path of awakening in itself. The Buddha said he taught only suffering and the cessation of suffering. By focusing our attention on the present moment, cultivating mindfulness shows us what we do that enhances suffering and what we can do to relieve it. Here are some of the reasons why mindfulness is an essential tool on the path of awakening.

Mindfulness Helps Free Us from Judgment

A key feature of mindfulness is nonjudgmental awareness of whatever experience is present for us. Judging involves evaluating our experience against some standard we set, which we then come to believe is "right." By contrast, nonjudgmental awareness enables us to impartially observe everything and everyone around us because we're free to experience each moment without imposing *shoulds* or *shouldn'ts* on it and without calling it good or bad.

We tend to expect many of our experiences to be either wholly joyful or wholly sorrowful. We're likely, for example, to believe that funerals must only be somber and weddings must only be joyful. These kinds of judgments often set us up for disappointment and suffering. As Zen teacher John Tarrant says in his book *Bring Me the Rhinoceros*, "Children laugh at funerals, some tears shed by brides are from disappointment rather than joy."

Keeping his words in mind, imagine attending a wedding or a funeral, having resolved in advance to put aside your judgments regarding joy and sorrow, and to simply pay attention to how the day unfolds. What would your experience be like without your "everyone should be joyful" or "everyone should be somber" mind set? Not only would you be free of the disappointment and suffering that follow on the heels of dashed expectations, but you'd be open to the rich and varied nature of each experience.

I've discovered that when I'm truly paying attention to my present-moment experience, I rarely have time to judge. As soon as I engage one moment, I've got to make way for the next one. It's such a relief to be free of the constant need to add *like* or *dislike* to my bare experience. Even if I can only sustain this for a moment, I know that I have the chance to do it again. We can go from the suffering of judgment to the freedom of no judgment over and over again, and mindfulness is our best tool for accomplishing this.

Mindfulness Offers Relief from Self-Focused Thinking

Of course, thinking is necessary a good part of the time—at work, in conversations, while planning our lives. But when we're not performing these kinds of tasks, our thinking can be relentlessly self-focused. We replay painful experiences from the past. We engage in a running commentary about our present-moment experience. We mock up worst-case scenarios about the future. The stories that we tell ourselves often serve only to increase our suffering. It's liberating to open our awareness to the world around us instead of always being preoccupied with our personal stories or with achieving our desired outcomes. This opening of awareness connects us in mind and body to all of our incoming experiences, from seeing the tiniest insect to hearing a noisy jumbo jet flying overhead.

When I catch myself lost in self-focused thinking, I take a deep breath and intentionally focus on one of the sense doors *other* than the ongoing chatter in my mind. As I take this breath, I recall Zen teacher Robert Aitken's story about his grandmother. She would take a breath and then give a big sigh as a way of sweeping her mind clear of what was troubling her so she could start anew. When I take this deep breath, I always think of that sigh. The sigh, the breath: both clearing out of the mind the suffering of self-focused thinking and opening us to receive the next moment with curiosity.

Mindfulness Enables Us to Reflect before We Speak or Act

Not only can our thinking be self-focused, it can also easily get us caught up in a chain reaction where one thought piles upon another until it gets hard to see clearly through the mental clutter. This is known in Buddhism as the proliferation of thoughts. Then, instead of being mindfully aware of what's going on in our minds from moment to moment, we feel overwhelmed and confused, leading us to speak or act without reflection. This makes us more likely to respond to others unskillfully, perhaps saying or doing something we may later regret.

When I first lost my good health, I vented my anger and frustration at many people who intended me no harm—from medical personnel to my own family. But the more I practiced mindfulness of the thoughts and emotions that arose in my mind, the more I became aware of my reactive tendencies. Now I'm better able to catch myself when I'm frustrated or upset at someone, take a conscious breath, and choose a more skillful way to respond.

Mindfulness Turns Mundane Activities into Richly Textured Moments

At meditation retreats, mindfulness outside of formal sitting meditation is a crucial component of the retreat. For example, everyone participates in "work meditation" so that the retreat will run smoothly. I would always sign up to put food away after meals. I'd perform the task slowly, so I could be mindful of the sights and sounds and physical sensations as I picked an appropriate container, put the leftover food into it, covered it, and put it in the refrigerator.

This might sound like a mundane activity, but with mindful awareness, work meditation became an opportunity to awaken moment to moment by being fully present and engaged in each task: deciding on the right-sized container for the amount of food that was left; transferring the food from the serving tray into the container without spilling it; noticing if irritation or self-judgment arose if I picked the wrong-sized container or spilled the food as I was transferring it; feeling the suffering in that irritation or that judgment. This intentional engagement with what was happening in the present moment generated curiosity and wisdom, not boredom.

You can try this by picking a simple activity that you perform every day. Some suggestions: showering, eating a snack, driving to work. Resolve to practice mindfulness during this activity. Perhaps you'll choose doing the dishes. As you're washing them, pay attention to the sequence of tasks and to the sights, sounds, smells, and sensations on your hands and your fingers.

At some point, your mind is likely to wander off from attending to these sensory inputs and get lost in thought: "I should have done a better job at the meeting this morning"; "I'm not prepared for tomorrow's class." If this happens, notice if self-judgment has arisen over this mental wandering and notice the suffering in the self-judgment. With practice, noticing without judgment that you've been lost in thought can itself be a moment of waking up to how things are: "Ah, I've been lost in thought and now I'm not!" When you're ready, return your attention to the warm feel of the water on your hands, the smell of the suds, the sight of a gleaming dish.

If you're thoroughly enjoying your chosen activity, notice if desire has arisen for it to last longer—even forever; that's impermanence dukkha from Chapter Five. Zen teacher Maureen Stuart expressed beautifully how understanding the truths of impermanence and suffering can turn mindfulness of everyday activities into an awakening practice:

> Life is suffering, the Buddha taught, because we want some permanency, some guarantee. If we let go of this desire and just follow a path of doing finite things in an infinite way, then ordinary becomes extraordinary; secular is sacred. Preparing the food, washing the dishes; everything is a sacred act.

Mindfulness Opens Our Hearts and Minds

The Tibetan Buddhist teacher Pema Chödrön refers to this as "Letting the world speak for itself." When I leave the house, I often use her phrase as a mantra: "Let the world speak for itself," I softly say to myself. Invariably, I find that the world answers with the full array of life's experiences—the smell of the rosemary bush right outside my front door, the valley heat hitting my face, the squawking of a scrub jay in the elm tree, the sadness of a child's sobs coming from the park next door, the sight of a young couple in love walking down the street.

Letting the world speak for itself is not an invitation to be passive. When we're engaged with our present-moment experience, it's clear when to take action to prevent harm to ourselves or another. Like all Buddhist practices, mindfulness is intended to alleviate suffering. We know when to abandon our calm and impartial observation and grab a child who's about to step out into traffic!

Moment-to-moment experience does not arise according to our desires. Sometimes the moment is pleasant; sometimes it's unpleasant. Cultivating mindfulness trains us to be calmly present for life's ever-changing joys and sorrows. This calmness of mind frees us from the suffering that arises when we cling to joy and resist sorrow.

Because unpleasant experiences are an inevitable part of life, mindfulness is not synonymous with joy: if you have a headache or have just fought with your partner or your children, careful attention to the present moment is not a joyful, pleasant experience. But mindfulness *can* be synonymous with waking up: *this is how things are.* Just this moment. Just this headache. Just this heartache. With practice, we can learn to respond to our experience with unconditional openness, even if that experience is painful—even if that experience breaks our hearts.

Opening to our experience in this way can be difficult—and I, for one, don't always succeed. When I became chronically ill, suddenly I found myself living day-to-day with flu-like symptoms and with deep sadness because I had to give up my career. Initially, I recoiled from this unpleasantness. Instead of acknowledging the presence of these unpleasant physical and mental feelings—"Just this aching body; just this sadness"—I spent my days insisting, "*Not* just this!"

But my resistance didn't keep the unpleasantness from being present. All it did was add the mental suffering of aversion to my aching body and to the sadness. Eventually I realized that the only way I could find peace and contentment in my life was to open my heart and mind to what I was experiencing in the moment. When I did this, compassion for myself arose and my suffering and dissatisfaction with life eased tremendously.

I think of mindfulness as a mirror that reflects whatever comes before it. Mirrors don't cling to pleasant experiences or reject unpleasant ones. On a retreat in the 1990s, Buddhist teacher Joseph Goldstein said, "From the perspective of mindfulness, it doesn't matter what arises." His comment made me realize that it is awareness itself that holds the promise for us to find peace—simply being aware of our moment-to-moment experience and having that be sufficient. What a gift it is to be human and have this potential!

8

Tools for Sharpening Your Mindfulness Skills

Waking up in the morning, I smile.
Twenty-four brand new hours before me.
I vow to live in each moment
and to look at all beings with the eyes of compassion.

—THICH NHAT HANH

MINDFULNESS PRACTICE—paying attention to your present-moment experience—sounds so enticingly simple and easy that you may be saying to yourself, "I'm going to do it!" That's exactly what I did many years ago. What followed was a honeymoon period during which I found it effortless and exhilarating to be mindful. I felt as if I were seeing the world through new eyes. My awareness of the three marks of experience was heightened, and I was much more engaged with my moment-to-moment experience. Then the practice lost its newness and the glow wore off.

Have you ever put an inspiring quotation on your refrigerator door and, for a while, every time you see it, you're inspired anew? Then comes the day when you look right past it as you open the door to grab some food. The quotation has become a bunch of meaningless words. So you replace it with a new quotation and the process begins anew. That's what happened to me with mindfulness practice. After a while, phrases like "be mindful" that had been so inspiring to me when I first learned them had become stale and formulaic.

Because of this, I decided I needed some mindfulness tools to incorporate into my everyday life. I was searching for concrete ideas that would create new habits and inject new life and energy into my mindfulness practice. These five tools have helped me tremendously.

Cut Back on Multitasking

The Korean Zen teacher Seung Sahn liked to tell his students: "When reading, only read. When eating, only eat." In other words, no multitasking. I wondered if doing one thing at a time would improve my ability to be mindful of the totality of the experience of that one thing. Unfortunately, as soon as I tried to implement this plan, I discovered that multitasking was my normal mode of operation. It was such a deeply ingrained habit that I had trouble even becoming aware that I was doing it. So learning to be mindful of my multitasking as it was happening became my first challenge.

Here are a few multitasks I caught myself performing: surfing online while talking on the phone; editing some writing while trying to follow a movie on TV; composing an email while listening to an audiobook *and* eating a piece of toast! It takes discipline to break the habit, so much in fact that sometimes I have to be content with "less multitasking." But I'm working on it. Call me a recovering multitasker.

I encourage you to become aware of when you're multitasking so that you can assess the effect it has on your ability to be mindful of your present-moment experience. Pick a day and resolve to notice when you're doing more than one thing at a time. If you're like me, this in itself will be a challenge. At the point that you *do* become aware that you're multitasking, stop and pick one of the tasks and stick to it alone for a while. See if you feel more fully engaged with your moment-to-moment experience. You may feel some anxiety as you "single-task." I've had that happen. I see it as a bit of desire-driven dukkha that I like to call multitasking withdrawal.

As you cut back on multitasking, don't expect perfection. When I get frustrated at my attempt to change this ingrained habit, I call to mind another Seung Sahn story that always makes me smile. A woman came into a room at his Zen Center in Providence, Rhode Island, and saw him eating breakfast while reading the morning newspaper. She said, "But master, you said that when eating we should only eat, and when reading we should only read!" He looked up and laughed: "When you eat and read, just eat and read."

Perform Tasks More Slowly

In April 2011, National Public Radio ran a story titled, "The Slow Internet Movement." It reported that hipster cities like Portland, Oregon, were sprouting internet cafés that only offered dial-up access to the web. These cafés offer customers "Slow pours and slow internet. Here, you can order your coffee and spend four hours checking your email, all for 99 cents an hour."

"Wow," I thought. "That's just my speed!" But the story didn't just run in April. It ran on April first and was NPR's little April Fools joke at the expense of gullible listeners like me. It got me thinking, though: embracing the spirit of the Slow Internet Movement might improve my mindfulness skills. By intentionally slowing down my tendency to rush through life, I might have a better chance to engage my moment-to-moment experience.

So as an experiment, I took the Slow-Internet-Movement-that-wasn't and applied it to everyday activities. I slowed them down by about 25 percent. I tried it with surfing the internet, feeding the dog, doing dishes, showering, doing the laundry. As was the case with cutting back on multitasking, this proved to be a tough challenge. I was so deeply conditioned to move at a fast pace that even though I'd start out at a reduced speed, unless I was vigilant, I gradually picked up my pace.

In deciding on tasks to practice with, I purposefully picked a few I didn't enjoy because I wanted to see if the heightened mindfulness that came from performing them more slowly made me more aware of my reactive mind. It did. One of those tasks was the dreaded laundry. Starting out at 25 percent reduced speed, the first thing I became mindful of was that aversion arose solely as a result of picking up the dirty clothes basket to begin the thirty second trek to the washing machine! By walking slowly though, I could see that this negative reaction was simply a habit of mind that served only to trigger unnecessary suffering and dissatisfaction. After all, the laundry must be done, whether I enjoy doing it or not. Slowing down gave me time to observe the entire mental process.

Once in the laundry room, I paid careful attention to each task in the process, from loading the machine, to shaking out the wet clothes, to putting them in the dryer, to folding them. I was keenly aware of how my senses were engaged: the smell of the laundry detergent, the sight of the crumpled clothes after the spin cycle, the warm feel of the dry ones in my hands. I wound up enjoying the task—and have ever since.

I can't say I've enjoyed all the tasks that I've tried at this slower pace, but that's fine because the purpose of this exercise is to sharpen our mindfulness skills, not necessarily to have a good time. Although I'm more likely to enjoy a task if I perform it mindfully, there's much to be learned even when the experience remains unpleasant. I watch the *don't-want* of aversion arise in my mind; I feel the suffering in that aversion; and, on a good day, I'm able to engage the task with wholehearted mindfulness, dislike included. The dog must be fed, like it or not: "Just this—just this feeding the dog."

I hope you'll try this slowing down practice. Pick one of the tasks that I chose or try others, like getting dressed, grocery shopping, maybe even playing with your kids. Hmm. That last one sounds like a challenge. See if you can get your kids or grandkids to play with you at 25 percent reduced speed!

This practice sharpens my mindfulness skills because, when I perform tasks more slowly, it grounds mindfulness in my body and I can feel all my senses perk up. I become acutely aware of sights, sounds, odors, tastes, bodily sensations, even thoughts and emotions. As a result, I'm much more attuned to my moment-to-moment experience. And sometimes the felt-need for that experience to always be to my liking drops away, leaving me content with my life as it is.

Stick to a Concrete Description

My daughter Mara introduced me to a practice from a remarkable teacher named Byron Katie. I altered it a bit so I could use it as a mindfulness practice. It's particularly effective if you're feeling stress of any kind. Begin by taking a deep breath and slowing down a bit. Then ground yourself in the present moment by concretely describing what you're doing and feeling right now, without intensifying it with loaded words, such as *awful* or *unbearable*.

Let's use loneliness as an example. Using this practice, if you were sitting at home, feeling lonely, instead of saying to yourself,

"Sitting at home, feeling unbearably lonely," you'd simply say, "Sitting at home, feeling lonely."

In expressive writing, words of embellishment—almost always adjectives and adverbs—are powerful tools for enhancing the meaning and emotional impact of a sentence. But if you're trying to just be present for what's happening in the moment, those words can add an emotional punch that leads you to begin spinning stressful stories about your life. When you leave out embellishments, such as *awful* and *unbearable*, you can mindfully (and compassionately) be with your present-moment experience without adding the suffering of storytelling dukkha—stories that take this form: "Sitting at home with a loneliness that will never go away"; "Sitting at home alone because nobody cares about me."

These stories not only add an extra layer of suffering to your present-moment experience of loneliness, they can also lead you to regard loneliness as a permanent part of who you are instead of the arising and passing mental state that your wisdom mind knows it to be. When you stick to the bare facts—"Sitting at home, feeling lonely"—without embellishing them, loneliness can become no more than what you happen to be experiencing at that moment.

I hope you'll try this practice. It may take some time to become adept at concretely describing what you're doing or feeling, while leaving out those emotionally-laden adjectives and adverbs that most of us habitually add to the bare facts of our experience. It's worth the effort though because this is a powerful tool for grounding yourself in the present moment.

Use a Mindfulness Bell

This is a mindfulness tool devised by the Vietnamese Zen monk and teacher Thich Nhat Hanh. On retreats at his monastery in Plum Village, France, a temple bell is struck every hour. Upon hearing it, the instruction is to stop and take three conscious breaths to bring yourself into the present moment.

Using a mindfulness bell is a great way to sharpen your mindfulness skills. Decide on a sound to serve as your "bell." Almost any sound will do—a horn honking, the purr of a cat, the thump of your refrigerator going off after its cooling cycle. Some people have a computer application that rings a tone at set or at random intervals. When you hear the sound you've chosen, stop whatever you're doing, take a few conscious breaths, and bring your awareness to your present-moment experience. The beauty of this practice is that you're bringing your mind and your body to the same place. That's true mindfulness.

My hound dog's bark is my mindfulness bell. I used to react with aversion to this sound. In fact, his bark was invariably followed by the sound of my yelling: "Rusty! Stop barking! *Now!*" Instead, that bark has become my signal to bring my attention to the present moment. If at all possible, I stop what I'm doing and take a few conscious breaths, feeling the sensation of the breath going in and out of my body. As I do this, I take in all that's happening in my field of awareness, from the bay of a hound dog, to a picture hanging on the wall, to a tinge of pain in my body, to a rush of emotion in my mind. Having taken it all in—feeling fully connected in mind and body to the world around me—I return to whatever I was doing.

If you find yourself becoming complacent about your mindfulness bell, pick another sound. So far, Rusty's bark has continued to work for me—and it's a relief to be greeting that bark with nonjudgmental mindfulness instead of the *don't-want* of aversion. But if I began to ignore the sound altogether or found myself thinking, "Oh there's the bark that's supposed to remind me to stop and come back to the present moment, but I'm present enough," that would be the sign that it's time to find another mindfulness bell. Just like replacing that quotation on the refrigerator.

"Gathas"

Gathas are short verses from the Zen tradition that direct our attention to what we're doing in the present moment. I invite you to discover them. Thich Nhat Hanh wrote a book of gathas called *Present Moment, Wonderful Moment*. His gathas cover everyday, routine activities. When I recite them, I become aware of everything about the task at hand, even its unpleasant aspects. Gathas can't make our day 100 percent pleasant, but they enhance our mindfulness of the present moment, and so they open us to life as it is. I also enjoy considering the reflections about life that Thich Nhat Hanh includes with each gatha. Here are his gathas for getting dressed and driving a car:

> *Putting on these clothes,*
> *I am grateful to those who made them*
> *And to the materials from which they were made.*
> *I wish everyone could have enough to wear.*

> *Before starting the car,*
> *I know where I am going.*
> *The car and I are one.*
> *If the car goes fast, I go fast.*

Zen teacher Robert Aitken's book *The Dragon Who Never Sleeps* contains a set of gathas I treasure deeply. In composing them, he followed a set form. The first line establishes *the occasion*, for example, "Watching the ants clean up the kitchen." The second line—"I vow with all beings"—is his personal vow, in which he's saying: "I vow and I yearn that all beings might vow with me." The third and fourth lines are his expression of how to meet the occasion with mindfulness and compassion.

When I read his gathas, I like to pause after the second line—the vow—and think about how I would finish the verse. I ask myself what words I'd use to express my deepest wish for all beings (including myself) to meet *the occasion* with mindfulness and compassion. Here are three of his gathas.

> *Watching the ants clean up the kitchen*
> *I vow with all beings*
> *to clean up the waste on my desk*
> *and the leftover crumbs in my head.*

> *When I stroll around in the city*
> *I vow with all beings*
> *to notice how lichen and grasses*
> *never give up in despair.*

> *When things fall apart on the job*
> *I vow with all beings*
> *to use this regretful energy*
> *and pick up the pieces with care.*

I hope you'll try writing and then reciting your own gathas. This is what I'm partially doing when I consider how I might finish Robert Aitken's verses. Any activity can become the subject of a gatha—brushing your teeth, eating your food, working at the computer. You'll get a mindfulness benefit times two. First, the act of writing a gatha is an exercise in mindfulness because, to write it, you have to pay careful attention to your present-moment experience. Second, whenever you engage in the activity that your gatha describes, the gatha will serve as a reminder to do so mindfully. Writing gathas and reciting gathas—both sharpen our mindfulness skills.

Each of these practices for sharpening our mindfulness skills calls on us to slow down a bit. When we do this, mindfulness becomes a doorway to awakening because we're looking more carefully at both our outer and inner experience. We allow all our sense doors to open, including the mind.

As each moment unfolds, we're better able to recognize where we grasp at and cling to pleasant experiences and where we reject unpleasant ones, and how these two *want/don't-want* reactions are sources of suffering. Mindfully seeing this enables us to wisely choose not to follow that initial impulse to cling to joy and to resist unpleasantness and sorrow. Instead, we engage—even embrace—the present moment *just as it is*.

9

From Multiple Hindrance Attack to Five-Minute Mindfulness

The real voyage of discovery is not in seeking new landscapes but in having new eyes.

—MARCEL PROUST

I VIVIDLY REMEMBER ONE summer day in 2011 as I sat in the lounge chair in my backyard. I was suddenly overcome with "I wanna get outta here." I was able to recognize it as a hindrance—restlessness—but I couldn't muster the mental energy to hold it in mindful awareness so I could investigate it. This was because I was also being visited by another hindrance—lethargy—which was manifesting as a feeling that I couldn't be bothered to check out what was going on in my mind. All I felt was "I wanna get outta here." Being mostly housebound, however, "getting outta here" wasn't an option for me.

As I continued to sit there, irritation arose, which is a form of yet another hindrance—anger. So now I had a full-blown multiple hindrance attack going! The irritation triggered stressful stories

—storytelling dukkha—which took the form of self-judgment: "You're always writing about being at peace with the present moment. What a fraud!" I can occasionally still be cruel to myself like this—but thankfully, as soon as I became aware of this negative self-talk, I saw the suffering I was inflicting on myself and made the conscious choice to stop it in its tracks by smiling at the silliness of this mental chatter.

Then, in an "all's well that ends well" tale, right there on the spot, I made up a practice that I've named *five-minute mindfulness*. You can do it almost anywhere—sitting outside (like I was), waiting for food at a restaurant, or even at work. The basic practice is to breathe normally and move your attention from one sensory input to the next, counting fifteen breaths during each part of the exercise. You can take more or fewer breaths—fifteen felt right to me. (If you don't have the use of one of the senses I cover here, focus longer on the physical sensations of the body.)

The purpose of counting breaths is to help keep your attention focused on the sensory input in question. Think of the breath as being like a railing that you hold onto in a stairwell. Like a railing, the breath keeps you steady and balanced in the present moment. And like a railing, you always know how to find the breath if you need to. This four-part exercise takes about five minutes. It starts with *seeing*.

Seeing

Rest your attention on everything you see. You can hold your head still or slowly look around. Take the world in with your eyes. Notice that your eyes are seeing shapes, colors, brightness, textures, and movements, but your mind immediately jumps in and attaches names to the objects of your perception—oak tree, cloudy sky, woman reading a magazine. This is natural. It's what the mind does!

At first, you'll see the objects that are most prominent. Soon, you'll begin to notice more subtle things, like the slight movement of the leaves in the breeze, tiny bugs floating in air, or a sad look on another person's face. When you become aware that your mind has wandered off into discursive thinking—"I wonder how long it will be until lunch is ready?"—return your attention to counting breaths and to taking in all that you see. (With this and the other three parts of the exercise, if you lose count, start over or just estimate where you were.)

The Buddha said, "In seeing, only seeing." That's the essence of this part of the exercise.

Hearing

Now do the same with hearing. You can close your eyes if you're in a place where that would be appropriate. Pay attention to everything you hear. Notice that your ears are hearing pitches, rhythms, and variations in volume, but your mind immediately jumps in and attaches names to the objects of your perception: dog barking; horn honking; airplane buzzing; people chatting.

When I practiced this in my backyard that summer day, at first, I only heard the most prominent sounds. By the time I got to the tenth breath, however, I was amazed at what I was hearing. I never realized there were so many sounds in what is considered to be a quiet neighborhood. I also noticed that there was a surprise element in the hearing exercise that wasn't present in *seeing*; I never knew what sound I'd hear next. This heightened my curiosity, which in turn heightened my mindfulness. As with *seeing*, if you realize that your mind has wandered off into discursive thinking, simply return to counting breaths.

The Buddha said, "In hearing, only hearing." That's the essence of this part of the exercise.

Feeling Physical Sensations of the Body

Now move to bodily sensations. When I did this in my yard, the first thing I noticed was the sensation of air coming in and going out of my nostrils. Then I became aware of the strong heart palpitations that I live with every day due to my illness. Next I felt the sensation of my jaw being clenched, so I relaxed it; that felt good. I also felt pain in my right shoulder. I acknowledged its presence and tried to relax into it. By not resisting the pain, I was able to keep secondary muscles around the point of pain from tightening. I just sat with the unpleasant sensation, without adding stressful thoughts about how long it might last or what it might mean.

From there, I moved on to the sensations in my body at each spot where it touched the lounger, and then to the sensation of my hands resting on my thighs. Suddenly I realized I could feel the slightest breeze on my face, something I'd been unaware of before starting the exercise. This was getting interesting! Even a slight itch in my eye had its charm.

The Buddha said, "In feeling physical sensations, only feeling physical sensations." That's the essence of this part of the exercise.

Take It All In

Open your eyes if they've been closed and, for fifteen breaths, become aware of everything appearing in your field of awareness: sights, sounds, bodily sensations, any tastes in your mouth or odors you might smell, any thoughts or emotions arising in the mind. The Buddha also said: "In tasting, only tasting; in smelling, only smelling; in cognizing, only cognizing." I left tasting and smelling out of the first three parts of this exercise, but now I've added them in.

When I was done with this practice, I checked out how I was doing. Was I still irritated? No. Was I still restless? No. Did I still "wanna get outta here"? No! I even felt energized instead of lethargic, as if I'd been on Marcel Proust's voyage of discovery.

Two Variations

In these two variations, instead of moving through several senses while counting your breath, focus on one sense for about five minutes. As with the exercise above, if you don't have the use of the sense of sight or sound, use bodily sensations instead.

Mindfulness of sights. Slowly looking around you, scan the entire field of vision available to your eyes. Let them take in what's in front of you, what's on either side of you, what's beneath you and above you. You can continue in this fashion for the entire five minutes, or you can focus your attention on one object of perception for a while, examine it in detail, and then move on to another object. You can also focus on the space between objects. If a sight is bothersome to you, note it as "unpleasant" so that, having acknowledged its unpleasantness, you can more easily let it be without resisting it or telling yourself stories about it.

Notice that your eyes are seeing shapes, colors, brightness, textures, and movements, but your mind attaches names to the objects of your perception. I like to intentionally let go of those names and try to experience what I'm seeing as visual waves—shapes, colors, brightness, textures—traveling through space and into my eyes. I hope you'll try this—but with a playful attitude. I can only do it for a short time before my mind jumps right in with a name.

I always come away from this exercise amazed at how much is present in my field of vision. When I don't intentionally practice mindfulness, I can be so lost in thought that my body processes visual data unconsciously. As a result, I don't even notice what I'm seeing or, if I do notice, I only see a fraction of what's available to my eyes.

For example, one day I tried this exercise while lying on my bed. If you'd asked me what was in my room before I practiced mindfulness of sights, I'd have mentioned only a small percentage of what turned out to be in my visual field of awareness. I have a Paul Cézanne print on the wall. It's been there for so many years that I'd stopped noticing its presence. But while doing this exercise, I mindfully examined "Still Life with Basket." It turns out, I'd never even noticed the name of the painting even though it's in big letters at the bottom of the print.

Mindfulness of sounds. Concentrate on sounds for five minutes. Close your eyes, unless you're in a setting where that would be inappropriate. Begin to take in the sounds around you. If a sound is bothersome to you, note it as "unpleasant" so that, having acknowledged its unpleasantness, you can more easily let it be.

Notice that your ears are hearing pitches, rhythms, and variations in volume, but your mind attaches names to the objects of your perception. Try hearing the sounds as vibrations traveling through space and into your ears. See if you can do this without attaching a name to the sound. Again, be playful with this. There's no reason to be discouraged if your mind jumps in and attaches a name. That's what minds do.

If the sound is someone speaking a language that you understand, your mind will do more than just name the sound, "person speaking." It will also translate the sound vibrations into language and meaning. In contrast, if a person is speaking a language you don't understand, then the sound of his or her voice will be more like that of a dog barking. Your mind will identify the sound as "person speaking," but it won't turn the sound into abstract concepts.

Whenever I start this practice, at first I hear only a few sounds— those that are the loudest or the most familiar to me. After a while, not only do I hear other sounds, but I hear nuances in those initial sounds that I hadn't noticed before. When I'm finished, I'm always surprised at how much turned out to be present in my auditory field of awareness.

I also feel a sense of expansiveness and openness to the world. (For this reason, I sometimes practice mindfulness of sounds for longer than five minutes, as a kind of formal meditation.)

One benefit of these practices is that they can be done almost anywhere. To others, you're just sitting or standing in an ordinary way. I've practiced five-minute mindfulness as a passenger in a car, while sitting in a waiting room, while standing in line, and while lying on my bed.

A second benefit is that it's a simple and effective way to add a formal mindfulness practice to your hurried life—five minutes at lunchtime, or before a meeting, or before the kids get home from school. It will leave you refreshed and ready to greet the rest of the day with curiosity, no matter what it has in store for you.

The essence of five-minute mindfulness is captured in this comment that Zen teacher Taizan Maezumi once made about life: "You're doing it anyway. You might as well appreciate it."

10

Choiceless Awareness

Freedom is found in the choiceless awareness
of our daily existence and activity.
—JIDDU KRISHNAMURTI

CULTIVATING MINDFULNESS is beneficial, whether inside or outside of meditation. That said, formal meditation practice sharpens our ability to pay attention to our present-moment experience and so makes us more adept at cultivating mindfulness when we're not meditating. There are many mindfulness meditation techniques. One is not superior to another; all of them can be doorways to awakening.

In one technique, a *single object of awareness* is used to help ground our attention in the present moment. We're instructed to focus our attention on this single object—often the physical sensation of the breath—and when we notice that our attention has strayed, we gently but firmly return our focus to the object. Using the sensation of the breath as the object of awareness is particularly beneficial for calming the mind. "Following the breath," as this is often called, may be the most common mindfulness meditation practice in the West. When I mentioned in the previous chapter that I practice mindfulness of sounds for longer than five minutes as a kind of formal meditation, I'm using the sounds around me instead of the breath as my single object of awareness. When my attention wanders or I get lost in thought, I return my focus to what I'm hearing. Using sounds as the object of awareness is particularly beneficial for developing a sense of expansive openness.

A second mindfulness meditation technique is termed *choiceless awareness* or *bare awareness*. In this technique, we begin by paying attention to the sensation of the breath (this settles the mind and body), but then the instruction is to let our attention rest on whatever is most prominent in our field of awareness. This is the meditation technique I'm going to cover because it best fits the theme of the book—awakening by engaging the whole of our experience fully, however it presents itself. In the quotation that begins this chapter, Indian spiritual teacher and philosopher Jiddu Krishnamurti uses the word "freedom" to describe this awakening.

As a meditation practice, choiceless awareness is similar to the Zen meditation technique known as *shikantaza*, which roughly translates as *just sitting*. I love the idea of just sitting, although for me, just lying down will do—which takes me to my number one rule regarding meditation: be flexible.

Flexibility

I learned the value of flexibility when I was the dean of students at the law school. As finals approached, I'd ask students to make a study schedule by filling in a calendar with subjects to study at given times each day. Then came my most important instruction: "Unexpected stuff will happen that will keep you from following this schedule exactly as you've created it. When this happens, don't throw it out. Just make a few adjustments and start following it again." I came up with this little speech because I learned early on that "throwing it out" was precisely what the students would do as soon as they weren't able to follow the schedule they'd initially created.

When I became chronically ill, I had my own schedule demon to face. It was an overly strict meditation schedule that I'd set in stone ten years before: sit upright in meditation twice a day for forty-five minutes each time, *no matter what*. I was so rigid about it that I insisted on meditating twice on my own children's wedding days! Unable to adjust this schedule to accommodate my illness, I quit meditating altogether. Ten years of meditating—and I threw it out. It took me ten years of illness to realize that I needed to be flexible. And so I've started meditating again. I lie down or half recline on my bed. I may meditate for ten minutes, for twenty, for forty. A testament to the value of flexibility.

Instructions for Practicing Choiceless Awareness

Pick a quiet place and a time when you won't be interrupted. Decide ahead of time exactly how long you plan to meditate because a restless mind is quite adept at coming up with any number of excuses to stop. Find a comfortable position—sitting on the floor or in a chair, even lying down. You can keep your eyes open but I suggest closing them, at least at first.

Start by doing a quick scan of your body, from the top of your head to your toes. Is your body tired? Is it full of energy? Is there any pain or other discomfort? For a minute or so, focus on the physical sensations of your body. The purpose of this is to bring your mind and body to the same place before you start the formal practice.

Now settle your attention on the physical sensation of your

breath as it comes in and goes out of your body. Find the place in your body where that physical sensation is the most prominent. It might be in your nostrils or at the back of your throat. It might be in the rise and fall of the abdomen. It might be in the expansion and contraction of your entire torso. It doesn't matter. Just rest your attention on the place where the sensations most strongly let you know when your breath is coming in or going out of your body. Recall from the last chapter that the breath can be thought of as a railing in a stairwell. As you practice choiceless awareness, if you need to settle and steady your mind in the present moment, you can always reach for that railing—the breath.

Once your mind has settled into feeling the physical sensation of the in- and out-breath, let go of your attention on the breath and open your field of awareness to all the sense doors. Keeping your mind open and alert to what's happening in the present moment, notice what is most prominent in your field of awareness. It could be a sound. It could be a sensation in your body. It could be mental activity in the form of thoughts, emotions, or images. Just watch in a relaxed and curious way where your attention goes.

Notice whether what is most prominent in your field of awareness feels pleasant or unpleasant . . . or neither. If it's pleasant—perhaps the sound of a bird singing—a feeling of joy might arise in your mind. Then you might find "really wanting it to continue" arise. This is the mind clinging to pleasant experience. It's a response that can carry a bit of anxiety with it—the suffering of impermanence dukkha—because, although you're enjoying the experience, you also know the bird could stop at any moment. Conversely, if what's most prominent in your attention is unpleasant—perhaps the sound of your neighbor's boom box—you might find that a resistant *don't-want* response arises in your mind. Just watch your *want/don't-want* mind with curiosity.

The beauty of this meditation technique is that, from the perspective of choiceless awareness, it doesn't matter what presents itself in your experience at any given moment. The Burmese Buddhist monk U Tejaniya, when teaching choiceless awareness, says: "Don't try to create anything, and don't reject what is happening. Just be aware." Thus there's no need to try and keep your attention on one particular object of perception, such as the breath. You're simply trying to stay alert to whatever arises in your field of awareness. All that matters is that you notice, including noticing your mind's response to what you notice!

If nothing is most prominent in your field of awareness, or if you become confused about what to do, simply return your attention to the physical sensation of your in- and out-breath—your railing. Then, when your mind feels relaxed and steady, let go of your attention on the breath and, once again, open your field of awareness to notice what is arising in your experience at the sense doors.

The Wisdom of Choicelessness

Choiceless awareness is not only a mindfulness practice. It's a wisdom practice because, with time, our wisdom mind will see clearly the three marks of experience: impermanence, no-fixed-self, and suffering or dissatisfaction.

We notice that nothing that arises in our field of awareness stays the same for long (impermanence). Experiencing this constant flux and transformation leads to the realization that there's no need to identify with bodily sensations or with thoughts and emotions as *me* or *mine* (no-fixed-self). This insight into no-fixed-self can give rise to a sense of great ease and spaciousness. Finally, by watching our response to pleasant and unpleasant sensory inputs, we come to know what experiences we cling to and what experiences we resist and how this gives rise to suffering and dissatisfaction.

Choiceless awareness meditation is a superb tool for getting to know our minds because we don't only pay attention to sounds, odors, bodily sensations, etc. We also watch the mind's response to them. On a retreat, Buddhist teacher Joseph Goldstein shared with us what the great Bengali meditation teacher Munindra once said to him: "If you want to know how the mind works, sit down and watch it." That's exactly what we're doing here.

Everything that presents itself in our field of awareness provides an opportunity to observe how our own mind works: When do we grasp and cling? When do we resist and reject? Seeing this, we're better able to simply be present, choicelessly, for our moment-to-moment experience. Coming to know the mind in this fashion opens the door to awakening to a peace and well-being that aren't dependent on whether a particular experience is pleasant or unpleasant.

Practice Note: Compassion Comes First

You may feel the urge to move due to physical pain or discomfort during meditation. The general instruction is to just be aware of the unpleasant sensation and to notice the aversive *don't-want* response in your mind. That said, sometimes it's wise to move if, for example, ignoring pain or discomfort could lead to an injury. I like the guidance given to us at a daylong retreat led by the British monk and teacher Ajahn Amaro. He told us to assess if the urge to move was stemming from self-concern and self-compassion, as opposed to the mind simply not wanting to put up with an unpleasant physical sensation any longer. He said that if the urge to move was stemming from the former, then . . . move!

Similarly, as is the case with any meditation technique, if troubling thoughts increase in intensity so that it becomes too stressful to watch your mind, out of compassion for yourself, please seek the assistance of a trained meditation teacher.

In both situations, trust your judgment and err on the side of compassion.

Practice Note: If a Sensory Input Is Overwhelming

You may find that a sound or other sensory input is so overwhelmingly unpleasant to you that you get stuck in aversion to it even after becoming aware of the suffering that your *don't-want* response is causing. This is aversion dukkha, and here's a story that might help.

Years ago, my neighbor had accumulated every conceivable power gardening tool known to humankind. My meditation space was close to his backyard. If I was meditating and one of those power tools started up—particularly the weed eater—it became the predominant sensory input in my field of awareness. But even *more* compelling than the sound of the gardening equipment was my aversion to it.

I tried to listen to the sound and watch in a relaxed and curious way the *don't-want* response that arose in my mind. But my irritation kept intensifying and eventually turned into full-blown anger at my neighbor. Soon I drifted off into storytelling dukkha: "I can't believe how inconsiderate it was of him to have bought that equipment"; and "That noise is ruining my meditation." Sometimes I got so angry that I stopped meditating—not without self-recrimination.

Then one day I was reading *A Still Forest Pool* by the Thai Buddhist monk and teacher Ajahn Chah. I came to a passage in which he was talking about noises and other sensory inputs that we think are disturbing us:

> In our practice, we think that noises, cars, voices, sights, are distractions that come and bother us when we want to be quiet. But who is bothering whom? Actually, we are

the ones who go and bother them. The car, the sound, is just following its own nature . . . Learn to see that it is not things that bother us, that we go out to bother them.

It was a revelation. I saw that I was creating my own suffering around those power tools. From then on, whenever I heard the weed eater, I'd note: "It's the nature of a weed eater to make a high-pitched whining noise." It simply became what was present in my field of awareness, and gradually I was able to greet it with curiosity instead of aversion.

Practice Note: If You Get Caught in a Thicket of Thought

I used to get frustrated when my mind would wander off during meditation and get lost in elaborate stories about the past, the present, or the future, even though I knew the instruction was to non-judgmentally notice the thoughts. Onto the frustration, I'd often add another layer of suffering in the form of negative self-judgment about my wandering mind: "Why can't you control your mind? You didn't put aside this forty-five minutes just to go over and over what you're going to say at tomorrow's meeting." (I tend to lecture myself in the second person.)

One day I was reading in one of my favorite books, *Mindfulness in Plain English* by Bhante Gunaratana. He was writing about the mind wandering off into thoughts during meditation. He said what I'd heard over and over: just notice the thoughts without judgment. My reaction was, "I know, I know; I've heard this dozens of times." But then I got to the next paragraph:

Somewhere in this process, you will come face to face with the sudden and shocking realization that you are completely crazy. Your mind is a shrieking, gibbering madhouse on wheels barreling pell-mell down the hill, utterly out of control and hopeless. No problem.

This is one of my favorite passages from all my Buddhist books. I don't know which of these three lessons I treasure the most: the comforting knowledge that, like everyone else, I'm completely crazy; the description of my mind as shrieking, gibbering, and hopeless; or the assertion that it's "no problem." When I read this passage, I immediately understood that this is how the mind is—inside and outside of meditation. Once I relaxed about my hopeless mind, it did indeed become "no problem" when it wandered off into thought during meditation. And when I stopped the negative self-judgment about that wandering, I could more effortlessly see the impermanent nature of this "gibbering madhouse."

There are two ways we can respond in that moment when we realize we're caught in a thicket of thoughts. We can respond judgmentally, as if it reflects poorly on us that we weren't able to keep our attention in the present moment. This is the "I'm not good enough" response that I referred to in Chapter Four as being foreign to the Dalai Lama. The alternative is to treat the realization that we've been lost in thought as a moment of awakening: "Ah, I was lost in thought. Now I'm not!" I'm working hard to cultivate this latter response. I see it as another one of those tasks that the Buddha gave us to work on as we walk the path of awakening.

II

Awakening to the Body through Mindfulness

*If one thing is developed and cultivated, the body
is calmed, the mind is calmed, discursive thoughts are quieted,
and all wholesome states that partake of supreme knowledge
reach fullness of development. What is that one thing?
It is mindfulness directed to the body . . .*

—THE BUDDHA

FROM THIS QUOTATION, we see that the Buddha considered mindfulness of the body to be a path of awakening in itself. For many years, I attended an annual Buddhist meditation retreat at which Gil Fronsdal was one of the teachers. Several times, he shared with us what the Thai Buddhist monk and teacher Bhikkhu Buddhadasa had said to him on a retreat: "Never do anything that takes you out of your body." I could tell that people found this to be very meaningful, but it never resonated with me. As an academic, I lived in my mind, not my body. I depended on my body for survival, but I had very little felt-sense of it.

Then I became chronically ill and the interconnectedness of the body and the mind became startlingly clear. My physical symptoms could affect my mental state. Indeed, at times, it seemed as if there were a direct link between my physical discomfort and the mental suffering of storytelling dukkha, because when I was at my worst physically, the stressful stories I spun and believed without question were always worst-case scenario themed.

In turn, my thoughts and emotions could affect my physical symptoms—easing or worsening them, depending on what was going on in my mind. I realized that by living in my mind all those years, I'd been ignoring half of the experience of being alive. If I were to recover my health, mindfulness of the body would remain an integral part of my life, inside and outside of meditation.

Mindfulness of the body refers to the cultivation of awareness at the sense door of bodily sensations. (We practiced this briefly in five-minute mindfulness.) The instruction is to become consciously aware of the physical sensations that arise in the body. This mindfulness practice is still the principal meditation technique taught at many Buddhist centers in Southeast Asia.

Body Sweeping

The Burmese meditation master and layman U Ba Khin taught mindfulness of the body using a technique called *body sweeping.* Meditators were instructed to sweep their awareness through the body, paying attention to physical sensations. Over time, the sense of the body as one solid entity gave way to experiencing it as an uninterrupted flow of changing sensations. This heightened a meditator's awareness of the first mark of experience.

According to U Ba Khin, thorough and ongoing awareness of impermanence was *the* path of awakening. If a meditator could truly see that everything that arises passes away, he or she would understand the futility of clinging to pleasant experiences or resisting unpleasant ones.

U Ba Khin inspires me to reflect deeply on impermanence and its relationship to awakening. If it's futile to cling to or resist what's happening in the moment because everything is subject to change, we might as well open unconditionally to our moment-to-moment experience. This embracing of what's present in the moment—known in Zen as *just this*—is an awakening. It's a moment of peace with our life as it is.

Mindfulness of the Body and Sensory Splitting

Mindfulness of the body can be practiced anytime and almost anywhere. If you're sitting in a waiting room or at your desk at work, you can bring awareness to your body. Try it. Begin by scanning your body for any areas of tightness, aching, or pain. If a sensation is unpleasant, rest your attention on it without aversion or judgment. When I practice mindfulness of the body, I purposely try not to name the body part in question or the nature of the sensation—pain, aching—so I can focus on the sensation itself. Invariably, what seemed at first to be a block of one sensation—*shoulder pain*—breaks down into an array of sensations: tightness, softness, heat, cold, vibration, pulsating, burning, tingling, waves of more intense and less intense sensation.

This separating out of sensations is called *sensory splitting*. It helps us recognize the three marks of experience—impermanence, no-fixed-self, and suffering. When we separate out the sensations, we realize that what we'd been thinking of as a permanent, solid block of tightness, aching, or pain is, instead, a variety of constantly changing sensations. This makes it easier not to identify with an unpleasant sensation as a fixed part of ourselves. Then we're less likely to react to it with aversion, and suffering doesn't arise.

For example, if I'm experiencing neck pain, my mind tends to jump right in with aversion (specifically, aversion dukkha—resisting an unpleasant experience): "Oh no, pain; I hate this." But when I use mindfulness to help with sensory splitting, what I was identifying as pain becomes a variety of sensations: tightness, burning, pulsating, waves of painful sensations—some more intense than others. By sensory splitting in this way, the pain no longer feels like one solid entity, making it easier to not identify with it. I'm also less likely to get caught up in stressful stories about it, such as "This pain will never go away." Without that stressful storytelling dukkha, my suffering is eased.

The Body Scan

In the West, Buddhist mindfulness meditation on the body often takes the form of *the body scan*. It's akin to U Ba Khin's body sweeping meditation and, like that technique, heightens our awareness of impermanence. The body scan is also a doorway to awakening because it helps us open to whatever physical sensations we're experiencing at the moment, without clinging to pleasant sensations or turning away in aversion from unpleasant ones.

Before going into detailed instructions, here is an overview of the body scan.

You'll be moving your attention from one part of your body to another. When you move to a new area, linger there, imagining that you're breathing into it and out of it. After some moments, mentally let go of that part of the body and move your attention to the next area. You may not feel any sensations in some parts of your body. That's fine; just notice, "not feeling anything." If a sensation is unpleasant, as you breathe into that part of your body, try sensory splitting. Then just let the sensations be, without attaching a negative judgment or any meaning to them. They're just sensations.

The idea here is to become more adept at experiencing bodily sensations *as* bodily sensations, without getting lost in the mind's reaction to the sensations. Of course, this takes practice. So when the mind does jump in with its analysis and opinions on the matter with thoughts such as "I hate this pain" or "This will never go away," as soon as you notice this has happened, acknowledge the presence of *don't-want* in your mind, and then return your attention to the physical sensations in your body.

When I experience unpleasant physical sensations while I practice the body scan, my mind often jumps right in with a negative reaction. But I've discovered that if I simply acknowledge the presence of *don't-want*, my mind often gives up its running commentary. Then I'm able to just experience the unpleasant physical sensation without adding an extra layer of unpleasantness in the form of aversion in the mind.

Throughout the meditation session, maintain an attitude of friendliness toward your body. After all, it's working hard to support you. Simply set the intention to be with your body with curiosity and kindness, and see what happens.

Body Scan Meditation

You might have someone read these instructions to you or record them yourself for playback.

Find a comfortable place to sit or lie down where you won't be disturbed. Put aside anywhere from twenty to fifty minutes for the body scan. The time you allot will affect how slowly or quickly you move from one area of your body to another.

1. Gently close your eyes and begin by resting your attention on the physical sensation of your breath as it comes in and goes out of your body. Breathing in, know you're breathing in. Breathing out, know you're breathing out.

2. Move your attention to the toes of your left foot. Imagine you are breathing into your toes and out from your toes. This may take some practice. It helps to imagine your breath flowing from the in-breath at your nostrils, down through your body and into your toes. Feel any sensations in your toes, or note the lack of sensation. If you feel pain or tension in your toes, try sensory splitting. Then let the sensation or sensations be, always with an attitude of friendliness and kindness. If your attention wanders off into thoughts, when you realize it's happened, gently bring your attention back to your left toes.

3. When you're ready, on the out-breath, mentally leave your toes and move your attention to the sole of your left foot, then to the heel and then to the ankle, following the same instructions as for the toes.

4. Following the same instructions as in #2, withdraw your attention from one area of your body and move it to the next area in this order:

- The lower left leg, including the calf, the shin, the knee;
- The left thigh—front and back—and its connection to the left hip;
- The right toes, the sole of the foot, the heel, the ankle, the calf, the shin, the knee, the thigh, the connection of the thigh to the right hip;
- The pelvic region and its organs;
- The abdominal region and the organs of the digestive system;
- The tailbone and then up the back from the lower to the middle to the upper back;

- The chest, including the heart, the lungs, the breasts;
- The fingertips of your left hand, the back of the hand, the palm, the wrist, the forearm, the elbow, the upper arm;
- The fingertips of your right hand, the back of the hand, the palm, the wrist, the forearm, the elbow, the upper arm;
- The shoulders and armpits, up into the neck;
- The jaw and then the teeth, the tongue, the mouth and lips;
- The cheeks and sinuses, the eyes, the muscles around the eyes, the forehead, the temples, the ears;
- The back of the scalp up to the top of the head.

If you want to practice for longer, you can now reverse the process and move from your head to your toes in the same fashion.

5. To finish the exercise, return your attention to your breath and become aware of your body as a whole, alive from head to toe with sensations. Send thoughts of friendliness and kindness to the body—this remarkable organism that sustains you in this precious life.

Because the body is a storehouse of both pleasant and unpleasant sensations, mindfulness of the body, whether inside or outside of meditation, is an opportunity to awaken to the sensations that exist in the present moment. In this way, we can engage our bodies fully, without clinging to pleasant sensations or resisting unpleasant ones. By becoming acutely aware of the ever-changing nature of bodily sensations, we can learn to be at peace with the body as it is at this moment in our lives.

Mindfulness of the body as a practice touches the three paths of awakening that are the subjects of this book. *Wisdom*: Mindfulness of the body brings impermanence and no-fixed-self to the forefront of our attention; it also enables us to see how clinging and resisting lead to suffering. *Mindfulness*: This practice *is* a form of mindfulness! *Open-heartedness*: Mindfulness of the body as a practice teaches us to open our minds to our present-moment experience; this, in turn, softens our hearts so that we naturally respond with compassion to any suffering we might be experiencing.

This is why the Buddha said that "mindfulness directed to the body" calms the body and the mind, quiets discursive thought, and that "all wholesome states that partake of supreme knowledge reach fullness of development."

12

Death Awareness Practice

Worlds on worlds are rolling ever
From creation to decay,
Like the bubbles on a river,
Sparkling, bursting, borne away.
—PERCY BYSSHE SHELLEY

IN THIS CHAPTER, we're going to explore, in a gentle way, what are called *death awareness practices*. If you're not comfortable with the subject matter, or are not ready to explore this topic presently, please feel free to skip this chapter. You might choose to skip it if you're mourning the recent death of a loved one or if you're feeling depressed right now. Trust your judgment. You can always return to the subject at another time. Had I encountered a chapter like this some years ago, I might have skipped it myself. Like many people, I'm not entirely comfortable thinking about death, even though it's been a part of my life since I was a young child. I lost both my father and my grandmother before my eleventh birthday. I was very close to both of them; Nana, as I called her, lived with us.

There are also some very good reasons not to skip this chapter—and these practices. To my surprise, I haven't found death awareness practice to be at all morbid. Not only is it preparing me for an event that inevitably awaits me and my loved ones, but becoming mindful of death is heightening my awareness of the wonder and mystery of my life right now. This is giving rise to a greater appreciation for the gift of each new day.

My Inspiration to Take Up Death Awareness Practice

I remember exactly what I was doing one summer day in 1993 when I had a life-changing experience. I was sitting in a hotel lobby in Honolulu, reading from a pamphlet I'd been handed at a nearby Buddhist temple. I'd reached a paragraph that described the meaning of tanha—the desire that makes us feel that we *need* to have everything turn out to our liking. Finishing the paragraph, I looked up at my surroundings and suddenly had an insight that if I were truly free of desire, I'd be content with the world: I would want nothing more from it than it is. As this insight arose, I experienced a brief moment of all desires dropping away. This gave rise to a feeling of deep peace and well-being. It was a profound spiritual experience for me.

About fifteen years later, I realized that my experience of the dropping away of desire on that summer day in Honolulu, profound as it was, was incomplete. This is because there's another aspect to tanha: the desire *to exist and continue to exist.* And so, to know complete peace, I'd have to be free of the desire to live for as long as I want. I'd have to be at peace with the prospect of dying. The realization that I was not *at all* at peace with this prospect inspired me to begin exploring death awareness practices.

Moreover, the Buddha thought that reflecting on death was important to prepare us for our own death and for the death of our loved ones. To this end, as part of his mindfulness of the body practices, he instructed his monks to go to the charnel grounds where bodies of the dead used to be piled prior to cremation—and to examine them, part by part, in various stages of decomposition. Then the monks were to contemplate: "This body of mine also has this nature, has this destiny, cannot escape it."

I'm not including meditations of that type here because I'm personally not comfortable doing them myself—though perhaps one day I will be. What's more, I'm not sure they'd be helpful for everyone. Instead, I'm going to describe four death awareness practices that I use myself and find to be beneficial. I recommend that you read through all of them and start by picking one or two to practice with. But first . . .

Practice Note: Working with Fear

What if fear arises as you're working with one of these practices? Many years ago, I had an intense experience with fear while participating in a death awareness practice. I was on a retreat led by Ayya Khema. Toward the end of the retreat, we came into the meditation hall and, without warning, she instructed us to contemplate the inevitability of our death. I wasn't prepared for this. I thought we'd just be sitting in meditation as we'd been doing for ten days.

As we sat, she repeated phrases for us to contemplate: "Death is inevitable. I don't know when it will come. No one is exempt." By the end of the period, I was so scared and upset that I returned to my room even though eating was next on the schedule. To my surprise, my roommate Tay was there. Seeing that I was in distress, she broke the silence and asked if I was okay.

I shared with her that the contemplation on death had frightened me. She immediately sat next to me on the bed and put her arm around my shoulder. She told me that what was scaring me was the *idea* of death, but that the idea of what death would be like was just a collection of thoughts and images that my mind was imagining. She went on to say that there was no reason to believe that these thoughts and images had anything to do with what the actual experience of death would be like. Then she pointed out that just because I was feeling fear right now didn't mean I'd be feeling fear when the time came.

As I listened to Tay talk, my fear gradually lifted. This compassionate woman who reached out to me in my suffering turned out to be one of my teachers on this retreat. Her words are still tremendously helpful to me, and I bow in gratitude to this woman whom I've never seen since.

And so, if fear arises during one of the four practices that follow, begin by treating it as your old friend fear—one of your regular visitors. Then reflect on what I learned from Tay—that the idea of death is not the same as the experience of death. The fear you're feeling is genuine, but don't assume it indicates how you'll be feeling when the time for death arrives. Working with fear in this way lessens its intensity and makes it manageable. Then just let the fear be until it passes out of your mind, while at the same time arousing compassion for yourself over the suffering you're feeling at the moment.

This Could Be My Death Day

This death awareness practice traces back to ancient Rome where it was called *memento mori*—remembering you will die. It's a mindfulness practice that encourages us to be aware of our own mortality. For a few moments every day, we are to think about the fact that this could be our death day.

I've been practicing this sporadically for many years. I'm working toward making it a daily reflection. Intentionally remembering that I will die is a skillful practice for me because when thoughts of death pop into my mind uninvited, I tend to get scared. It could be a thought about my own death or the death of a loved one. For example, one of my recurring uninvited thoughts is, "One day, this will be my last morning." When this thought arises without warning, it jolts me and I feel afraid. But when I intentionally think, "This could be my last morning," I react differently. Because I've invited the thought to arise, instead of my body and mind tensing up in fear and aversion, I treat the thought as a truth to be acknowledged, gently and with compassion.

And sometimes, having intentionally welcomed this reflection, a feeling of warm appreciation arises—appreciation for this morning in which I am very much alive! These are special moments and they inspire me to continue with this practice.

Goodbye Forever

At a meditation retreat in the late 1990s, Buddhist teacher Mary Orr told us about a practice she devised for when she takes leave of people she's close to. As they're saying their goodbyes, she silently says to herself, "Goodbye forever." This reminds her that there's no guarantee she'll ever see this person again. I was attracted to this practice but, because I was still experiencing a lot of fear about death, I decided to start in a modest way. So, in 2002, I began to use it with my elderly dog, Winnie.

Even this was a bold step for me. Soon after my father died, my mother brought home a puppy to help ease my pain. Not surprisingly, I formed a tight bond with my beagle, Connie. Since then, I've always insisted on having a dog in my life, even though the death of each one was traumatic. I wanted to try Mary's practice, so I started with Winnie. Every time I left the house or settled in for sleep at night, I'd look at her and say, "Goodbye forever." At first, fear arose as I said these words. But after a few days, instead of fear, I felt appreciation for the joy this creature had brought me for so many years.

One day, it did turn out to be goodbye forever. Because of this practice though, I was able to accept her death with grace compared to how I'd reacted to the loss of my other dogs. In the past, I'd get a surreal feeling that their death hadn't really happened. This "magical thinking" was a kind of denial. It was very painful and could last for weeks.

When Winnie died, however, my experience was dramatically different. Because I'd been saying "goodbye forever" to her every day for several months, I'd gradually come to accept that it was inevitable that the day would come when we'd be separated. Although I cried and was terribly sad when she died, at the same time, I felt an unexpected peace and well-being because I'd come to understand her death as part of the natural cycle of life and death.

The past few years, I've occasionally practiced this when I take leave of family members (they're finding this out for the first time as they read this). Sometimes when we hug and I silently say, "Goodbye forever," I feel fear arise. But at other times, my heart fills with love and appreciation for them. And so, I'll keep working with Mary's practice because I have faith in its benefits.

The Mystery of Death's Time

"Death has many causes and the time of death is uncertain." This reflection combines two of nine contemplations on death that were devised by the eleventh-century Buddhist sage Atisha. It has also been very helpful to me. When my father died of leukemia at the age of fifty, I was only ten, and so I learned at an early age about the unpredictability of death. He was the youngest of three siblings and was an adored family member. Everyone thought of him as the baby in the family, even after he was grown and had children of his own.

His family struggled to accept that "death has many causes and the time of death is uncertain." At the time of his death, over a decade had passed since the 1945 atomic bombing of Hiroshima and Nagasaki. Nevertheless, his family became obsessed with the idea that his death was due to radiation having blown over from Japan to Los Angeles. When I think back to what it was like as a ten-year-old to be at family gatherings after his death, I remember feeling bewildered about why they were so angry and bitter about that bomb. I simply wasn't able to empathize with the deep suffering they were experiencing over their inability to accept that sometimes "the baby" of the family dies first.

I don't know why my father got leukemia. Maybe it *was* due to the atomic bomb, although I doubt it. But if he hadn't gotten leukemia, he might have died in an auto accident, so there was never any guarantee that he'd outlive his older siblings. That is the mystery of death's time.

We tend to think that the people we know will go through childhood, adulthood, old age, and only then encounter death—and so it's not so hard to accept the death of a loved one when it occurs at the age of ninety. But it can be tremendously difficult to accept when it occurs before old age. My teacher in this regard has been the actress Susan Saint James.

Several years ago, I saw her interviewed on *The Today Show*. Three weeks before the interview, her fourteen-year-old son Teddy was killed in a plane crash. Her husband and another son were seriously injured and several of the crewmembers died. Saint James talked about how close she was to Teddy because he was her youngest child and the only one still living with her. Her husband's work kept him from being home very often. She said that she and Teddy were like roommates and had become best friends. Then, emanating deep calm and acceptance, she said: "His was a life that lasted fourteen years."

When I heard her say this, for the first time in my life, I felt at peace with my father having died so young—and while I was so young. I said to myself, "His was a life that lasted fifty years." I reflected on all the things we did during our ten years together and was able to feel that his life was complete and whole. I no longer felt cheated by him for having left me when I was ten—a feeling that had been a source of considerable guilt for me over the years.

I don't know if I could speak the words that Saint James did should my own children or grandchildren die before I do. But I'm practicing, and this contemplation has helped. I'm coming to accept that one of the conditions of being alive is that we are subject to innumerable and unpredictable causes of death. More and more, I'm willing to accept this as a condition of life and to treasure each day that I'm alive and that those I love are alive.

Grasping Dissolves at the Moment of Death

Several years ago, I came across a passage written by the Tibetan Buddhist scholar Robert Thurman. It struck me like a bolt of lightning, so much so that I copied it out by hand and have kept it nearby ever since. From his words, I devised this phrase to use as a death awareness practice: "At the moment of death, all that I'm grasping will be of no use."

Here's what Professor Thurman wrote:

> Tibetans observe that anyone can die at any time in any place . . . All the somethings in and around us with which we preoccupy ourselves from morning to night are potentially nothing to us. If we died, they would dissolve in our

tightest grasp, forgotten if they were in our mind, lost if they were in our hand, faded into blank numbness if they were our mind and body.

To practice with my phrase and with this passage, I become mindful of what I'm grasping at, no matter how petty it seems. I like to watch the singing competition *The Voice*. When I find myself grasping at an outcome—"Katrina just has to win!"—I think about how, should I die that night, that opinion would be of no use, *forgotten in my mind*. Or I look around my room and notice things I consider to be my possessions. Then I think about how, should I die that night, those things would be of no use, *lost in my hands*.

I reflect on how everything I preoccupy myself with will dissolve at the moment of death—all my opinions that I consider to be so important, all my worries about the future, all the material stuff around me that I think of as mine. All that grasping. Gone. Gone. Gone.

To me, there's nothing nihilistic about this reflection. On the contrary, I find it to be life-affirming because it motivates me to seriously consider what *is* important to me in life—and it's not my opinions or my worries or my possessions. Speaking personally, what I value most is my relationship to other people. Do I make myself available to them when they're in need? Do I listen with an open mind? Am I patient and caring? Do I try to help as best I can?

This death awareness reflection is also life-affirming because it moves me to ask this question: If all I'm grasping at will be lost at the moment of death, what might I do with my life that *won't* be lost when I die? This question has the power to inspire me to choose how to live. Perhaps after I've died, someone will remember how I reached out to them when they were in need and that will cause them to do the same for someone else. Perhaps the unconditional love I feel for my children and grandchildren will have taught them how to love in that way.

If you're comfortable with this particular practice, I encourage you to use it to reflect on how you might answer both of the questions I've just posed. What do you value most in life? What might you do with your life that won't be lost when you die?

And finally, I often end this practice by saying to myself: "If at the time of death all that I'm grasping will be of no use, why not stop grasping now?" This contemplation transforms this death awareness practice into a liberation practice. I imagine letting go of everything I'm grasping at—my opinions, my possessions, my identities, even this mind and body. Then, with all the welcoming friendliness I can muster, I look around and embrace the world as it's unfolding right at this moment.

If death awareness practice is new to you, I suggest that you start by picking one or two to work with—whichever ones resonate most with you. My experience with these practices is more positive than I imagined.

Integrating death awareness into my life is making me more comfortable with the prospect of death. It's also making me feel more connected to others. We all share this fate and so, if fear arises when I think about death, I know I'm not alone; this is very comforting. And I also feel compassion for others' fears about death, in the same way Tay felt compassion for me.

Finally, living with conscious awareness of death is making each day more meaningful to me. I feel as if I'm living more purposefully and that I'm more open to my moment-to-moment experience—awake to life as it is. Just this moment. Just this.

Cultivating an Open Heart:
Kindness, Compassion, Appreciative Joy,
and Equanimity

13

The Psychological States of Awakened Beings

I am larger, better than I thought;
I did not know I held so much goodness.
—WALT WHITMAN

WE CONTINUE on the path of awakening by cultivating four open-hearted mental states that are collectively known as the *brahma viharas*: kindness, compassion, appreciative joy (that is, rejoicing in another's joy), and equanimity.

There has been no shortage of attempts to translate brahma viharas into English. Some examples: the heavenly states; the radiant emotions; the limitless thoughts; the divine abidings; the four immeasurables; the boundless abodes; the sublime states. Translated from Pali, brahma vihara refers to *the dwelling place of awakened beings.*

Dwelling place is a physical metaphor for where the mind of an awakened being would dwell. And so it's a metaphor for the psychological state of mind in which an awakened being would engage the experience of being alive. No wonder we struggle to find the right words to translate brahma viharas. We're searching for a phrase that describes the most profound psychological states that humans can achieve.

I'll be referring to them as the *sublime states*. I like the word *sublime* because the dictionary defines it as "of such high spiritual or ethical worth so as to inspire awe." However, I encourage you to keep the other translations in mind as we explore these four mental states and the practices we can use to cultivate them.

There's no need to be intimidated by the words sublime, divine, heavenly, radiant. If you're thinking, "I can't possibly experience a mental state with such a lofty name," recall that awakening is not a one-time deal. We have the potential to awaken again and again. Every moment that we meet our experience with kindness, compassion, appreciative joy, or equanimity is a moment of waking up because we're engaging life as it is in the highest spiritual and ethical way possible.

And when we fall back into our painful mental habits—wanting, anger, resentment—we can start again. As I've said before, we can go from dukkha to no dukkha—from suffering to awakening— over and over again. With practice, these four psychological states hold the promise for us to be able to sustain awakening, moment after moment after moment.

The sublime states are so vital to our ability to flourish as loving, caring human beings that, going by other names, they are an integral part of most (perhaps all) religious, spiritual, and humanistic traditions. I'll introduce them here and then explore each of them further in separate chapters.

Kindness and Friendliness

Kindness and *friendliness* are two translations for the Pali word *metta*. I'll be using both words because each has its own feeling-tone. Indian sage Neem Karoli Baba expressed the essence of metta when he said, "Don't throw anyone out of your heart." It's important to recognize that this includes yourself. It also includes that relative who is a thorn in your side and the politician whose positions you abhor. We cultivate metta by working to respond to *all* beings with kindness and friendliness.

This can be a challenge. I don't always feel kind and friendly toward people, especially those who hold views with which I vehemently disagree. But I've learned from years of practice that cultivating metta when I'm feeling this way is a balm for my heart. As an example, I'll use a certain radio personality whom I find to be particularly aggravating. If I simply call him to mind, I don't feel friendly or kind toward him at all, but I also feel stress and tension in my mind and body. So I try to cultivate metta for him—that is, I try *not* to throw him out of my heart. In doing this, I've found a few reflections to be helpful.

First, I think about how, like me, he wants to be happy and free from suffering. Second, I reflect on how there are people in his life whom he cares about and treats with kindness. Taking this a step further, I feel sure that he and I share similar hopes and dreams for our loved ones—that they be happy and at peace with their lives.

These reflections soften my heart just enough so that, instead of getting stuck in anger and aversion toward him because of his views and inflammatory style, I become attuned to the qualities we share as human beings. This makes it possible for me to cultivate metta for him even though I don't agree with what he's saying or the style in which he says it.

Gaetano Donizetti composed an opera called *L'Elisir d'Amore*—the elixir of love. I think of metta as an elixir for my heart. It's a medicine that helps to heal any irritation, anger, or negative judgment that I may be feeling for myself or for others. It's a medicine that opens my heart so that I'm not afraid to wish the best for others even if I don't care to be in their company.

I suggest that you begin metta practice by cultivating it for strangers. I call this *friendliness practice*. Although we love our family and friends, we may also have some difficulties with them. By contrast, our relationship to strangers is relatively conflict-free. This makes it easier for us to feel the effects of evoking metta, and that's a good first step in becoming adept at cultivating this sublime state.

To practice, as I turn the front doorknob to leave my house, I consciously resolve to maintain an attitude of friendliness toward all the strangers I see. If I'm in a car and I see people walking on the sidewalk or driving next to me, I silently say something friendly to them, such as "Have a wonderful time today." If I'm waiting in line, I look at each person around me (unobtrusively, of course) and silently say to each one: "May you enjoy this day"; or "I hope you have fun today." I say whatever feels natural to me at the moment. Sometimes a negative judgment starts to arise when I first look at someone (isn't it amazing how easily we can judge people we don't even know?). When this happens, I silently say something friendly to that person anyway, and the judgment usually vanishes.

Cultivating kindness and friendliness can put us in touch with a sublime feeling of (nonromantic) love. Along these lines, Buddhist teacher Sylvia Boorstein once said that she practices metta by just looking at a person and silently saying, "I love you." When she shared this, I thought, "I can't do that!" But I've tried it and I can. When I do, I'm able to experience genuine love for complete strangers. I become acutely aware that we share this life with its joys and its sorrows and that we share this planet with its beauty and its troubles.

By the time I get home after greeting all of my experience with friendliness, the world looks a bit brighter to me and I definitely feel friendlier about the people in it.

Compassion

Buddhist texts describe compassion as the quivering of the heart in response to the recognition of suffering. To cultivate compassion, we become aware of the suffering in ourselves and others, and we do what we can to alleviate it. It helps to start with ourselves. Responding to our own suffering with compassion not only eases our pain, but gives rise to compassion for others because, as the Tibetan Buddhist teacher Pema Chödrön said: "Sorrow has the exact same taste for all of us." And so, when we truly see our own suffering, we're able to recognize it in others.

Treating others with compassion is a gift you can give of inestimable value. Think of some time in your life when you were suffering and someone reached out to you, showing that he or she understood your pain. Can you recall how it made you feel? I can think of a time this happened for me. A week or so after my father died, I had to return to my sixth grade classroom. I didn't want to go. I was embarrassed to be the kid whose father had died. I wanted to blend in and be treated like everyone else but was afraid that wouldn't happen. And I was right. My fellow students were awkward around me, being simultaneously too nice and too distant. I remember wanting to flee in misery.

My best friend, Janie Lakes (later to become Congresswoman Jane Harman), recognized my distress. She pranced right up to me, gave me a big slap on the shoulder and, using her affectionate nickname for me, said: "How 'ya doin' meatball?" It immediately relieved everyone's discomfort. I suddenly felt at home in my classroom, and my classmates felt at home with me. In one bold move, Janie relieved everyone's suffering and discomfort!

This story illustrates that compassion for others can be expressed in a variety of ways—some of them quite unconventional. So long as your intention is to ease others' suffering, you're on the mark.

One of the easiest ways to begin cultivating compassion is to practice it when you're in a place with people you don't know personally. It could be an airport or a park or a waiting room. I've tried it in all of these places. As I gaze at the people around me, I reflect on how some of them may have health problems and some of them may be mourning the loss of a loved one. Others may be nervous about an upcoming job interview or be worried about their children or an aging parent.

I think about how they, like me, must live as best they can with their ten thousand sorrows. Although the specific facts surrounding what has led to their individual suffering may differ from mine, we've all experienced sadness, worry, insecurity, and unhappiness. Having become attuned to their suffering, I evoke compassion for them, knowing that they, like me, want to be happy and at peace. To do this, I silently speak to them with phrases that express my deepest wish that they be free from suffering. Here are some of the phrases I use:

- ▸ I hope you have people in your life who care about your suffering.
- ▸ We share this planet and our suffering; know that I care.
- ▸ May your suffering ease soon.
- ▸ May you be as well as possible.

The last phrase is an expression often used by those living with chronic pain or illness. We even shorten it to "May you be *A WAP.*" But I like to address this phrase to everyone around me, because everybody has his or her share of stresses and sorrows—in sickness *and* in health.

As I did with metta, I've suggested that you start your compassion practice by focusing on strangers because these are people with whom you're unlikely to encounter conflict. When you're ready to expand your practice to those you're close to, I recommend that you begin by regarding them as you did those strangers—as people with whom you simply share this planet. The best way to do this is to drop the identities you've attached to them: mother, father, partner, child, best friend. Let them become people who, just like you, want to be happy and at peace. From this benevolent state of mind, you'll be better able to hold them with compassion in your heart, wishing that they be free from suffering, even if your relationship with them is imperfect.

Remember, whatever we repeatedly "think and ponder upon" becomes the inclination of our minds. And so, the more we cultivate compassion, the more it becomes our natural response to the world.

Appreciative Joy

When we're feeling appreciative joy, we rejoice when another person is joyful or happy. If we think of compassion as reaching out to relieve another's suffering, appreciative joy is reaching out to share another's happiness. Here's the clearest illustration I know. My friend Martha is blind. One day, she was out with a friend in the early evening. Suddenly, her friend began talking excitedly, her voice bubbling with pleasure at the sight of a beautiful sunset. Martha, of course, saw nothing. But she said that it genuinely made her happy to experience her friend's joy. Appreciative joy is a sublime state of mind that's available to all of us. The Buddhist word for it is *mudita*. In a sense, appreciative joy is also a compassion practice for ourselves, because tapping into our reservoir of joy takes us out of our self-focused thinking and, in doing so, eases our own suffering.

Appreciative joy can pop up in unexpected places. In March of 2012, Tony and I were watching the Academy Awards. When Octavia Spencer won the Oscar for Best Supporting Actress for her role in *The Help*, it was clear from her reaction that she didn't expect to win. When she got to the microphone, she was so overcome with joy that Tony and I turned to each other with smiles on our faces. In a delighted voice, he said: "Mudita!" There it was— simple and uncomplicated joy in her joy.

We may not have a one-word translation in English for mudita, but I'm happy to report that neither do we for the German word *schadenfreude*, which means feeling joy in the misfortune of others. I wish I could say that I've never felt schadenfreude. I have. But since I began practicing appreciative joy, I've noticed that the slightest movement of my mind in the direction of schadenfreude intensifies my own suffering, and so I rarely take joy in other people's misfortune. This has been an unexpected blessing of cultivating appreciative joy.

If this practice is new to you, I suggest that you start by cultivating appreciative joy for people with whom you have an uncomplicated relationship so that no obstacle, such as envy, sneaks into your rejoicing in their happiness. So, as with metta and compassion, try starting with strangers. Your goal at first is just to feel what it's like to experience joy in another person's happiness or delight.

Pick a day when you'll be going to a place where you can observe people, or pick a live television show—a talk show, a sporting event, an awards show. When you see people enjoying themselves—

smiling or laughing, talking animatedly with someone, rejoicing in a victory—let their joy fill your heart until you feel joy just because they're feeling it.

Appreciative joy is a simple practice, but a beautiful one. It frees us from suffering because we can't simultaneously be sharing joy with another person *and* be self-absorbed in the type of desire that is the source of suffering.

Equanimity

The fourth sublime state is equanimity. Cultivating equanimity helps us learn to greet whatever is present in our experience with an evenness of temper, so our minds stay balanced and steady in the face of life's ups and downs. This is a tall order, especially because it means engaging our lives with calmness and ease amid both pleasant and unpleasant experiences. Grasping at what is pleasant sets us up for impermanence dukkha because change is inevitable. And resisting what is unpleasant serves only to add stress to what is already a difficult situation.

For me, the greatest challenge in cultivating equanimity has been to let go of my self-appointed role as "the fixer." In the movie *Michael Clayton*, George Clooney plays a fixer. When his law firm makes a mess of a case, it's his job to make the problem go away. As soon as I heard the term *fixer*, I thought, "Oh no, that's me—always trying to fix my loved ones' lives so they won't have to experience those ten thousand sorrows."

When my children were young, I tried to protect them from suffering, as I imagine most parents do. The Buddha's father did. As the story goes, he tried to shield the young Siddhartha from being exposed to any suffering in the world, going so far as to post guards to keep him from leaving the royal grounds. But as a teenager, Siddhartha dared to venture forth and, for the first time, was exposed to human suffering. I'm grateful for his courage because that experience set him on the quest to find the answer to why we suffer and how we can find relief from it.

Like Siddhartha's father, I tried to shield my children from the sorrows of the world. And I thought I could fix all their difficulties. If something wasn't right at school, I was on the phone with the teacher. If there was a conflict with a friend, I was on the phone with the kid's parents. I thought I'd change when they grew up and started households of their own, but I didn't. If one of them had a cold, I regaled them with every possible remedy—even though they hadn't asked for advice.

With the Buddha's help, I'm a recovering fixer. I've come to understand that this continuous effort to protect my loved ones from the full range of life's experiences is not triggered by *their* suffering, but by my own—suffering that stems from my desire to fix their lives so they'll always be happy. Through equanimity practice, I'm learning to let go of this need to shield them from all disappointment and suffering. I'm coming to accept that everyone must be left to experience his or her own life, with its ups and downs and its joys and sorrows.

To help me with this practice, I silently recite equanimity phrases, such as:

- I love you, but I cannot keep you from experiencing suffering.
- Your happiness and unhappiness depend on your actions, not on my wishes for you.
- May you live in peace regardless of your circumstances.
- May you accept with grace both your successes and your disappointments.

As for my own ups and downs, I try to greet each day as it unfolds, knowing it won't meet all my expectations and knowing that most of my desires will go unfulfilled. The key to equanimity is understanding that life is an ever-changing parade of pleasant and unpleasant experiences that we rarely control. The self-focused desire of *want/don't-want* mind leads us to try and control our lives by fixing everything to be to our liking. But it never works, leaving us feeling disappointed and dissatisfied.

To practice equanimity, I resolve to be mindful of how my experience feels to me during a set period of time—maybe fifteen minutes. If an experience is unpleasant—too loud in a restaurant or too hot outside—I acknowledge the unpleasant feeling and then say to myself: "It's loud, but that's okay—restaurants are sometimes loud"; or "It's hot outside but it's the nature of the weather to sometimes be hot and sometimes be cold." If an experience is particularly pleasant—delicious food, a garden in bloom—I say to myself: "I'll enjoy this experience while it lasts, knowing that, like all phenomena, it will pass away and another experience will take its place." When I practice in this way, I'm able to touch the peace and well-being that come from connecting with my moment-to-moment experience just as it is, without the burden of always trying to change it.

I also practice equanimity toward the people in my life. Our interactions with others are inevitably a mix of pleasant and unpleasant experiences. On the unpleasant side, people don't always fulfill our expectations or keep their promises. In these circumstances, I cultivate equanimity by saying to myself: "I feel let down, but this is what people are like—sometimes they come through for us and sometimes they don't."

I have a friend who always promises to visit when she comes to town. I put the dates on my calendar, but she rarely calls. I don't call her because I know she has a lot of friends and family in town—she raised her children here—but I feel sad as I watch those dates on my calendar pass without a call from her. Once she's home, I get an apology email from her and a promise to visit next time. I practice equanimity over this disappointment by repeating phrases such as "I feel let down, but disappointments are part of life." I work on acknowledging my sadness without judging her negatively because, in my experience, that only adds another layer of suffering to my disappointment and sadness.

Practicing equanimity in these ways helps me accept that not all my experiences will be to my liking and not all people will behave as I would prefer. Acknowledging this helps me engage life more fully whether it happens to feel pleasant or unpleasant at the moment. Because equanimity fosters in us feelings of peace, contentment, and well-being, we experience our life as sufficient just the way it is without the constant need to fix it.

Wisdom and the Sublime States

Wisdom and the sublime states support each other. Cultivating wisdom facilitates the arising of the sublime states. And cultivating the sublime states deepens our wisdom. Each creates the conditions for the other to arise. Here's how.

Cultivating wisdom opens the door to the sublime states because wisdom attunes us to the human condition—that it's impermanent, with no fixed self, and subject to suffering and dissatisfaction. In focusing on these *marks of experience*, the Buddha was pointing to what we all have in common. When we understand that not always getting what we want is a universal human experience and how suffering arises when we fight this fact, we're able to feel how others suffer, too, when they fight it. And so we see ourselves in others, and we see others in ourselves. This makes it easier for us to open our hearts to all beings. Here are two examples of how wisdom helps us evoke the sublime states. First: compassion.

I clung with my wanting mind to my profession as a law professor long after I was too sick to reasonably continue working. As a result, I suffered greatly, both physically and mentally. Now when I hear about people who've lost their jobs either because of health difficulties or because of the downturn in the economy, my heart spontaneously reaches out to them with compassion. That compassion comes from knowing with my wisdom mind how much I suffered due to not being able to get what I wanted professionally.

Cultivating wisdom can also give rise to equanimity when we're disappointed about a particular outcome—perhaps not getting a job we'd hoped for. When we understand with our wisdom mind that not always getting what we want is a universal human experience, it's easier to accept disappointment with grace. Equanimity is the ability to open our hearts and minds to our experience as it happened, even if it didn't live up to our hopes and expectations.

On the flip side, cultivating the sublime states deepens our wisdom because intentionally evoking kindness, compassion, appreciative joy, and equanimity attunes us to how we and others are feeling. This makes it easier for us to see our own and others' suffering, and to recognize the desire that underlies it.

For example, in the face of my friend who lets me down by not contacting me when she's in town, I cultivate equanimity by trying to maintain an evenness of temper—that calmness of mind that knows that sometimes life turns out as we'd hoped and sometimes it doesn't. When I practice in this way, I see clearly that the suffering I'm experiencing is due to not getting what I wanted. But I also see that my friend is suffering too, because she cares for me and knows that she makes promises to me that she doesn't keep. Of course, I always hope she'll visit; but I don't want her to suffer over not visiting (which is why I always try to respond with compassion when that email apology comes). And so, cultivating equanimity gives rise to wisdom—in this particular situation, awareness of both my own and my friend's suffering—and then wisdom gives rise to compassion for both of us. This is an example of the reciprocity of wisdom and the sublime states.

Practice Note: Encountering Resistance

Cultivating the sublime states is a skill that takes practice, like learning to play a musical instrument or to speak a new language. Some days, practice will go better than other days—but even when practice is hard, it's worthwhile. Perhaps especially then.

Sometimes we resist responding with kindness, compassion, appreciative joy, and equanimity to whatever is going on in our lives. It could be because we're feeling overwhelmed by our own problems. It could be that we're feeling overwhelmed by other people's problems. This can happen to me. Some days, I become exhausted physically and overwhelmed emotionally from reading emails sent by people who've read my first book, *How to Be Sick*, and who, with the best of intentions, write to me at length about the serious difficulties they're facing in life. When my inbox gets too full, sometimes I can feel resistance arise—resistance to sharing their suffering. I just want to turn away.

When this happens, first, I acknowledge the presence of aversion in my mind—the *don't-want* of tanha. Next I work on evoking compassion for myself over how I'm feeling, recognizing that everyone feels overwhelmed at times by the suffering in the world. I find that if I don't address myself with compassion in this way, negative self-judgment is likely to arise over my inability to feel kind and compassionate toward others.

Finally, to help my heart open to the people who've written to me, I bring to mind how I felt when I was a child and someone was kind and compassionate toward me. I hope you'll try this when you find yourself encountering resistance to cultivating any of the sublime states. Let the warm feeling of someone treating you kindly and compassionately, or perhaps rejoicing in your joy, fill your heart and mind. The person I bring to mind is my nana.

She lived with us when I was a young child. No matter how tough a day I'd had, I knew that if I went to her room, she'd put down whatever she was doing and invite me to sit on her lap. We didn't even talk about my day. I'd just sit on her lap and let her kindness enfold me. And so when I'm feeling too overwhelmed to respond with compassion to those emails, I recall how I felt in my nana's lap. That inspires me to treat others the way she treated me. Then, when I'm ready, I return to my inbox and do my best to help ease the suffering of those who've written to me.

So if resistance arises when you begin to cultivate any of the sublime states, try acknowledging the resistance without negative self-judgment. Remind yourself that all of us feel too overwhelmed at times to reach out, perhaps even to ourselves. Then call to mind a person from your past who might be able to help you open your heart to yourself and others.

These four profound psychological states contain several common threads. First, when we cultivate them, we are committing ourselves to be active as opposed to passive in life—to be friendly, to be compassionate, to look for joy, to find peace and contentment with our life as it is.

Second, with all four, we are resolving not to harm anyone, including ourselves, so we're committing to relieving suffering in the world—our own and that of others to the extent we can.

Third, when we cultivate the sublime states, we are gradually transforming ourselves into an awakened being because every moment we respond to our experience with kindness, compassion, appreciative joy, or equanimity, we strengthen our inclination to respond that way again.

Finally, when people see us behaving in this way, we are modeling that behavior for them, making it more likely that they, in turn, will cultivate the sublime states. This ripple effect spreads outward and has the potential to touch everyone's joys and sorrows.

14

To Cultivate an Open Heart, Set Aside Judging

People take different roads seeking fulfillment and happiness.
Just because they're not on your road doesn't mean
they've gotten lost.

—H. JACKSON BROWNE

MY FRIEND JOAN likes to joke that dying will be a relief because it will put an end to the heavy burden of judging. She says she envisions herself in the moment before death, lying in a hospital bed, looking at the paint on the ceiling and formulating her last judgment: "What a hideous green."

I love her expression, *the heavy burden of judging.* Judging is an obstacle to waking up because it's hard to engage life as an awakened being—with kindness and friendliness, compassion, appreciative joy, and equanimity—if we're always adding *likes* and *dislikes*, *shoulds* and *shouldn'ts* to our bare experience.

Sticking to the Facts

There's a difference between assessing and judging. Assessing is a neutral sizing up of people or our environment by sticking to the facts we've been presented, whether those facts please us or not. Judging is what we add to assessing when we measure those facts against some standard we've set up regarding how we think people or things *should* be. So in judging, there's an element of dissatisfaction with the way things are and a desire to have things be the way we want them to be—enter our old friends dukkha and tanha.

Zen teacher Joko Beck recommended a practice to help us become aware of whether we're assessing or judging:

> Whenever we say a person's name, notice whether we have stated more than a fact. For example, the judgment, "she's thoughtless" goes beyond the facts "she said she'd call me and she didn't."

Sometimes the difference between assessing—sticking to the facts—and judging becomes apparent from the tone of our thoughts or voice. For example, I have a friend who is a nonstop talker and a friend who is a nonstop complainer. To think or speak in a neutral, purely descriptive tone, "She can talk nonstop for twenty minutes," is an example of assessing; assuming the description is accurate, I'm simply describing her behavior. On the other hand, to think or speak in a negative tone, "She can talk nonstop for twenty minutes," is an example of judging because that negative tone reveals my dissatisfaction with how she is and my implied desire for her to be different.

The same analysis applies to my complaining friend. If I say, "He complained about his life the entire time we were together," depending on my tone, it could be a neutral observation (an assessment) or it could reflect my dissatisfaction with him and my desire for him to be different (a judgment). Setting aside judging doesn't mean we have to actively seek out the company of people we don't enjoy or who treat us poorly. But we can decide whether or not to be with them without adding a negative judgment. This opens the door for us to cultivate the sublime states even for someone we don't want to spend time with. We can genuinely feel, "I wish for you to find peace and contentment even though I won't be hanging out with you."

If there's someone you're judging negatively at the moment, either because he or she let you down in some way or because of some personality trait that bothers you, try using Joko Beck's approach and write a description of this person that's an assessment, not a judgment. Let's say, for example, that you're upset with a coworker for not meeting a deadline. Here's how you'd describe what happened as an assessment: "He said he'd get me the material by Friday and he didn't." Here's how you'd describe it as a judgment: "He's so irresponsible and thoughtless that he can't even make a deadline."

Judging in this manner may turn out to be insensitive and unfair (perhaps your coworker is worried about a sick child or simply lacks the organizational skills to meet a deadline). In addition, adding the judgment "irresponsible and thoughtless" to the bare facts of the missed deadline gives rise in your mind to the second hindrance— anger—and the suffering that accompanies it. This anger may well prevent you from seeing that some constructive action on your part could keep this incident from happening again. Indeed, if you were to approach the issue by treating your coworker with the kindness and friendliness that characterize the sublime state of metta, he or she is unlikely to get defensive, making it more likely that the two of you could work out a satisfactory way to prevent a second missed deadline.

Judging Can Intensify Suffering

One summer about fifteen years ago, I learned the hard way how judging can be a recipe for suffering. Just as I was about to leave town to attend a ten-day retreat that included practicing the four sublime states, I received an email from the dean at the law school. The subject was my teaching load for the fall semester. Instead of neutrally assessing the bare facts in the email (a proposed teaching load for me), I decided that the email contained a negative judgment on the dean's part about my willingness to teach my fair share.

Thinking that he was judging me negatively, in turn, I judged him negatively. I went on the silent retreat (which turned out to be anything but silent in my poor tortured mind) and spun so many stressful stories about that email, it's embarrassing to recall. Soon I added a second layer to my judging. I began judging myself negatively for letting the email upset me while I was on retreat: "You're ruining your retreat by thinking about that email all the time."

This second layer of judging served only to intensify my suffering, leading me to feel isolated and separated from those around me. As a result, I wasn't able to evoke the sublime states for myself or for anyone else. I wasn't feeling friendly or compassionate or appreciative. And I certainly wasn't feeling the peaceful contentment of equanimity.

As soon as I got home, I called the dean. It turned out that he was concerned that my teaching load was too *heavy*. When I re-read his email, I could see that it very well could have been interpreted that way. I hadn't just judged; I'd misjudged what were, on his part, entirely good intentions. I look back on that incident and see a lot of unnecessary suffering on my part.

I've misjudged some doctors, too. One doctor I saw about my illness was thorough in his examination but seemed subdued and passive in his interactions with me. I interpreted his behavior to mean that he didn't want to have anything to do with a patient whom he might not be able to "fix." I discovered at a later appointment that I was wrong. He shared with me that he felt inadequate as a doctor because he wasn't able to help me. That got my attention because that's how I'd been judging myself—as inadequate for being sick and not knowing how to get better.

I'd been so caught up in blaming this doctor for his lack of enthusiasm that it never occurred to me that we might be sharing the same thoughts and emotions about my illness. So I learned once again that judging only increases my own suffering and unnecessarily separates me from others, making it hard to forge a genuine human connection.

Cutting Off Judgment

Two teachers from the Zen tradition have offered powerful teachings on setting aside judgment. The Korean Zen teacher Seung Sahn liked to instruct his students to keep a *Don't-Know Mind* so that they wouldn't become attached and cling to their views and opinions. He expressed this open-mindedness this way: "If you keep a Don't-Know Mind, then your mind is clear like space and clear like a mirror."

The Vietnamese Zen monk and teacher Thich Nhat Hanh offers his own gloss on Don't-Know Mind. He encourages us to always ask, *Am I Sure?* before we believe our immediate perceptions. He likes to use the example of how we panic if we see a snake in the dark, but when we shine a light on it, we see that it's only a rope. He suggests that we write "Am I Sure?" on a piece of paper and tape it to a place where we'll see it often. (Note that asking "Am I Sure?" is a very effective way to question the validity of those stressful stories we continually tell ourselves—our old friend storytelling dukkha.)

We can use both Don't-Know Mind and Am I Sure? to cut off

judgment as soon as it arises. Looking back on the incident with the dean's email and the way it affected my retreat, I wish I'd had these two practices to call upon every time I began to judge the dean. I could have reminded myself that I wasn't sure what he intended, so I might as well wait until I got home to get it clarified. And I wish I'd thought, "Am I Sure?" before concluding that the doctor I saw was uncaring.

In practicing Don't-Know Mind and Am I Sure?, it helps to recall the second mark of experience: no-fixed-self. When I believe that I'm fixed in permanent identities—parent, law professor, author—I tend to cling tightly to the views and opinions that I've developed to go along with those identities. Then I become *I think I know mind*. This gives rise to that judgmental mentality, "I'm right and you're wrong," which is the stressful story that's almost always behind the hindrance of anger. But when I drop these fixed identities, I'm able to engage people with an open mind. It's liberating to recognize that I don't know for sure that I'm right and others are wrong. Dropping judgment is indeed dropping a big burden!

There Can Only Be One Beatles

Judging others is often accompanied by judging ourselves. We seem all too adept at becoming the object of our own judging minds. This especially tends to happen when we compare ourselves to others and come up short in our estimation. Then *we* become the focus of our dissatisfaction with how things are, as we direct those *shoulds* and *shouldn'ts* at ourselves. This is the realm of the inner critic—a habit that afflicts almost everyone I know.

When I first started teaching, I compared my performance in the classroom to that of my colleagues. I even graded myself—a solid B+. Although I had many colleagues who rated lower than a B+ on my scale, I didn't give them a second thought. All I cared about were those whom I thought were better teachers than I was, and I judged myself negatively for not being in what I considered to be the A range. This was a source of much suffering for me. I even considered leaving my position.

One day I shared my unhappiness with my friend Guille who had no connection to the law school. She looked me straight in the eyes and said dryly but sternly: "There can only be one Beatles. That doesn't mean other people shouldn't make music." From that moment on, I began to enjoy my time in the classroom and was content with the quality of my teaching. I've shared Guille's comment with others to help snap them out of their self-induced suffering over their inability to be perfect at something. Her words never fail to have the same effect on them as they had on me.

Transforming a Negative Judgment

I've devised a metta practice to help me turn judging others into an opportunity to connect with them *human being* to *human being*. Even though I think of myself as a relatively nonjudgmental person, I'm amazed at how often I find myself engaged in petty judgments. I might make a snap judgment as I pass someone on the street: "She could stand to lose some weight"; "He shouldn't talk so loud on his cell phone." When I catch myself doing this, immediately, I silently say something kind and friendly to the person.

I love the effect that switching from judgment to metta has. The judgment dissolves and I feel a deep human connection to others because I'm wishing for them what I wish for myself. As a bonus, this practice gives rise to equanimity because I feel at peace with myself and with this person just as we are.

To try this practice, settle on a kind and friendly phrase. Some possibilities are: "Be well"; "Take care"; "Have a lovely day." Before starting the practice, resolve to be mindful of when you're judging others. Then as soon as you notice that you're judging someone, silently say your metta phrase.

When I first started this practice, it didn't feel genuine, and that may be the case for you as well. I kept at it, though, and now, not only does it feel genuine, but I'm often a step ahead of myself and can cut off the judgment before it's fully formed. Then I truly feel the relief that comes from not judging.

The World Contains Multitudes

As we've seen, it's hard to feel kind and friendly, compassionate, appreciative, or equanimous toward ourselves or others when we're judging. Walt Whitman wrote, "I contain multitudes." I like to think of the world as containing multitudes. I do this by consciously thinking: "This world is big enough for both the talkative and the untalkative; for both the complainers and the noncomplainers; for both those who come through for me and for those who let me down."

Accepting people as they are in this way opens the door to cultivating all four sublime states. Evoking *kindness and friendliness* for them—wishing that they be happy even if we don't want to be with them—is the essence of metta. Thinking of the world as big enough for the talkative, the complainers, and even those who let us down opens our hearts to feeling *compassion* for any suffering they may experience as a result of their behavior.

And to the extent that they're happy with the way they are, we can feel *appreciative joy*—joyful for their happiness. Finally, the image of the world containing multitudes—and of that being okay—gives rise to *equanimity* because when we engage people as they are, instead of clinging to the way we think they should be, we feel a sense of calmness and ease.

When we're not judging other people, our hearts are free to open to them and their suffering, and we're better able to see that, like us, they just want to be happy and at peace.

Judging others is such a deeply ingrained response that I often don't notice when I'm doing it, so I know I have a lifetime of conditioning to overcome. But it's worth it because judging and being able to cultivate the sublime states are like oil and water; they don't mix.

I truly hope I can shed that heavy burden of judging *before* that moment in the hospital bed when I'm staring at that "hideous" green ceiling.

15

Kindness and Friendliness

The highest form of wisdom is kindness.
—THE TALMUD

IN CHAPTER THIRTEEN, we looked at cultivating kindness and friendliness (metta) in an informal setting by silently greeting strangers with phrases such as "May you enjoy your day." Now I'm going to describe metta as a formal, structured practice. The origin of this practice traces back to a discourse the Buddha gave to his followers. The discourse contains this sentence:

> Even as a mother protects with her life, her child, her only child, so with a boundless heart should one cherish all living beings.

All living beings? The Buddha has set the bar high! But, after all, when we cultivate the sublime states, we're aspiring to engage our experience as would an awakened being. I like to have that bar set high, not to test myself, but to give me something to aim for—cultivating a heart so open and boundless that I feel as if I'm protecting all living beings from suffering, in the same way I would protect, with my life, my own children.

Instructions for Structured Practice

In this practice, you settle on a set of phrases and then recite them silently, over and over. You can practice metta during a regular meditation period, or you can put aside several minutes at set times of the day to recite your phrases. I recite my phrases before I get out of bed in the morning and again in the afternoon. These are the phrases I settled on in the early 1990s:

> *May I be peaceful.*
> *May I have ease of well-being.*
> *May I reach the end of suffering . . .*
> *And be free.*

There's no reason for you to use these particular phrases. Their cadence and meaning just work for me. *Ease of well-being* is a phrase I learned from Buddhist teacher Sharon Salzberg. I like it because it serves as a prompt to undertake my everyday activities with kindness and friendliness: "May I have ease of well-being as I dress . . . as I do the dishes . . . as I'm stuck in traffic . . ." Be sure to choose phrases that have meaning for you. Ask yourself, "What do I most sincerely wish for myself and for others?" Here are some possible phrases (I'll put them in the first person, even though you'll be addressing them to others, too):

- May I treat myself and others kindly.
- Let my mind be content with how things are.
- Let me make friends with my body.
- May I find peace and well-being.

Contrast these sample phrases with those that ask for a particular outcome that is either beyond your control to affect or that denies the full range of human experience and emotion. For example, wishing that people will always be nice to you expresses a desire for an outcome that you don't control and so is likely to lead to frustration and disappointment with metta practice. Similarly, wishing that you'll never have bodily discomfort or feel grief denies the existence of experiences that are part of the human condition, and so these types of phrases are also likely to lead to frustration and disappointment.

Try out different phrases and then settle on three or four that express most deeply your intention to cultivate kindness and friendliness toward yourself and others. As you begin to practice, feel free to change a phrase if it's not working for you. Moreover, if the sentiments expressed in your chosen phrases don't feel genuine at first, the traditional instruction is to recite them anyway. The idea is to incline your mind toward metta by revisiting the phrases and the intentions they express, over and over again. Gradually, your heart will soften and open to the sentiments you are expressing.

Traditionally, metta phrases are evoked for five specific people drawn from five different categories: yourself, a benefactor, a beloved person, a person about whom you feel neutral, and a person you find difficult.

YOURSELF

If you encounter resistance when trying to evoke kindness and friendliness for yourself, this is the realm of the inner critic that we looked at in the last chapter. Most of us have been conditioned to be highly self-critical and many of us have internalized a painful sense of unworthiness. If this applies to you, I hope you'll take to heart these words from the Buddha when he was asked about this very difficulty: "If you search the whole world over, you will find no one dearer than yourself." We can't always control the world outside of us, but we *can* learn to control our inner world, by which I mean how we treat ourselves and how we regard ourselves. In my view, there's never a good reason not to treat ourselves with the same kindness and friendliness that we treat those who are most beloved to us, and there's never a good reason to regard ourselves as unworthy.

Also recall that the Buddha said the mind is as soft and pliant as a balsam tree. This means that we can transform it from critic to ally. If you feel the presence of the inner critic when you recite your phrases, just include the critic as an object of your metta practice. In other words, address your inner critic with kindness and friendliness, even if your words don't feel genuine. Repeatedly reciting your phrases, while keeping in mind the intentions behind them, will gradually transform your tendency to judge yourself into a tendency to think of yourself in a warm-hearted way. The inner critic will weaken and, perhaps, just fade away.

A BENEFACTOR

The benefactor is someone for whom you feel deep gratitude. He or she might be a grandparent or an influential teacher in your life. The idea here is to pick someone with whom you have no conflicts. Some people pick a beloved public figure, like the Dalai Lama. With the benefactor (and with the people in the groups that follow), bring an image of the person's face to mind, or silently say his or her name—or do both; then recite your phrases, keeping in mind that the sentiments are intended for your benefactor. I always recite my phrases for Thich Nhat Hanh.

A BELOVED PERSON

Call to mind someone whom you love even though—unlike as is the case with your benefactor—there may occasionally be conflicts between you. This will be your beloved person. Although it's traditional to pick only one person to say your phrases to, I say mine to my husband, then to my two children, then to their spouses, and then to my grandchildren.

A NEUTRAL PERSON

The neutral person is someone in your life for whom you don't have strong feelings one way or another, like someone at work or a checker at the supermarket. If you stick with the same person each time you practice, over time, you're likely to find that this person becomes someone you really care about. It's a beautiful side effect of practicing metta for a neutral person.

Our mail carrier is my neutral person. For years, if I happened to see him though the living room window, my relationship to him was to focus on the stuff in his hands, hoping for that rarity—a handwritten letter. Then one day, after several years of picturing his face as I repeated my phrases to him during metta practice (*May you be peaceful . . .*), a shift occurred. I was in the living room as he was coming up the walkway to my house and my heart filled with affection and appreciation for him. I had to stop myself from throwing open the door and giving him a big hug!

A DIFFICULT PERSON

Call to mind a person whose name alone can give rise to aversion and irritation in you. It's best not to start with someone who might stir painful emotions, so begin with a person who doesn't pose a great difficulty for you. He or she could be a family member or friend with whom you have repeated conflicts, or a public figure with whom you disagree. If you find yourself getting anxious or angry while addressing your phrases to the difficult person, stop and switch to someone who's a milder source of annoyance.

To make it easier to practice with the difficult person, you might begin by reflecting on how this person, like you, wants to be free from suffering. The Buddha encountered many people who wished to do him harm. He responded not in anger but with kindness, because he understood the suffering a person must be feeling in order to want to harm another.

Because I've been practicing metta for many years, I usually go straight for my edges. I purposefully pick someone I feel disrespected by or with whom I vehemently disagree. It may be someone I know personally or it may be a public figure, such as a politician or political commentator. Wishing for a person who is a thorn in my side to be peaceful and to be free from suffering may be a challenge, but it turns metta practice into a liberation practice because it opens the door to freedom from the suffering that accompanies judgment and anger.

How to Handle Resistance

You can move through all five people during one session, or you can cultivate metta for just one person for the entire time period. On retreats that focus on formal, structured metta practice, it's common to spend several days—or weeks, depending on the length of the retreat—addressing your phrases to the same person.

The traditional instruction is to repeat your phrases in the order I've presented them: yourself, the benefactor, the beloved person, the neutral person, and then the difficult person. But I encourage you to feel free to recite the phrases in any order that feels most beneficial to you.

I also encourage you to listen for your response as you say the phrases. On a retreat, Sharon Salzberg once said to us: "The power of metta is so great that it brings up everything that stands in its way." And so, if you encounter resistance as you try to evoke metta for a particular person, regard it as an opportunity to investigate your aversion.

You should even feel free to stop the repetition of the phrases in order to go through the four-step approach for working with stressful and painful mental states. First, *recognize* that aversion has arisen. Second, *label it*, perhaps with "resisting feeling friendly toward him," or "not wanting to practice metta for her." Then *investigate it*.

Investigation might provide some insight into why aversion has arisen and whether the reasons for it continue to serve you well. Perhaps you have a list of complaints about this person and reciting your phrases made that list pop right up. If so, you might consider how wanting this person to be the way you think he or she *should* be is a source of suffering for you. Seeing clearly your wanting mind and how it leads to suffering can help ease that suffering.

Finally, if the resistance remains after you've explored it, just *let it be*, and return to your phrases with an attitude of understanding and tenderness for yourself over any suffering you might be experiencing.

Informal or Structured?

In informal friendliness practice (from Chapter Thirteen), we cultivate friendliness toward whomever we happen to encounter during the day. By contrast, in metta as a structured practice, we repeat our phrases by calling to mind the same people every day. (Of course, you should feel free to change to a new person if that feels better to you.)

Both practices have their benefits. The first practice leaves me feeling better about the world and the people in it. It gives rise to a joyful sense of open-hearted friendliness and curiosity. Structured metta practice, by having me repeatedly evoke my phrases while calling to mind the same people over and over, gives rise to a feeling of deep-seated and heartfelt benevolence toward them (as evidenced by my having to restrain myself from hugging the mail carrier!).

In both practices, we're learning to incline our minds toward kindness and friendliness until this sublime state becomes a natural response to our experience.

As are the other sublime states, metta is a skill that takes repeated practice to master, so be patient. The effort is worth it because every moment that we truly feel kind and friendly toward ourselves and others is a moment of freedom from suffering. That's why the sublime states are *the dwelling place of awakened beings*.

16

Compassion:
Start with Yourself

*The most difficult times for many of us are
the ones we give ourselves.*

—PEMA CHÖDRÖN

MANY PEOPLE FIND it hard to cultivate compassion for themselves. Recently, a woman wrote to me, saying that she couldn't be kind to herself because she was too accustomed to—as she put it—"beating myself up." I reminded her that the Buddha said our minds are soft and pliant and this means we can change our conditioning, no matter how ingrained it is.

I told her that if she couldn't stop "beating herself up," that was one more thing about which she could evoke compassion toward herself. I suggested that she address herself by silently or softly repeating this phrase: "It's hard to try and treat myself kindly when I'm so conditioned to beat myself up." I said that this kind of gentle self-talk could begin to untie the knot of that painful conditioning.

She wrote back to say that the phrase helped so much, she was using it as her new mantra.

My point is that there's no limit to what you can feel compassion for yourself over—even your inability to be self-compassionate!

Transforming Your Inner Critic

Recall the story from Chapter Four when the Dalai Lama was surprised to learn that Westerners disliked themselves. This kind of negative self-judgment was foreign to his culture. If you're like me, you were conditioned from childhood to judge yourself at almost every turn. When my health didn't return after the viral infection in 2001, I became my own harshest critic. Before I got sick, I made my living in a lecture hall. Now *I* was the captive audience—the recipient of the most mean-spirited lectures in which I ordered myself around in the second person as if I were a drill sergeant at basic training:

"You look like a fool at the law school for not recovering enough to teach."

"You've ruined your family's life with this stupid illness."

"You *will* get up tomorrow not feeling sick."

As Buddhist teacher Jack Kornfield likes to say: "The mind has no shame." I was trying to force my life to conform to how I thought it *should* be, even though these were circumstances over which I had no control. At the same time, I was judging myself negatively for being in those circumstances. This was fertile ground for guilt—the feeling that I'd failed my obligation to the law school and to my family.

It took me years to realize that talking to myself in this way not only added unnecessary mental suffering to the physical suffering of the illness but also made my physical symptoms worse. (After all, emotions are felt in the body.) And so, I finally decided to change course by beginning to cultivate compassion for myself. In other words, I resolved to recondition my mind.

I started by working to become mindful of the presence of this "drill sergeant." I was aiming for mindfulness without judgment. Setting aside judgment meant I had to treat the inner critic as a guest—even though an uninvited one. This neutral stance enabled me to investigate what was behind the painful and stressful thoughts that the critic was generating. It didn't take me long to see that the source of this stressful thinking was tanha: the desire to have my health restored—a desire so intense that I'd come to believe that fulfilling it was necessary to my ability to ever be happy again.

Recognizing this desire was eye-opening for me. As is so often the case when we're caught up in desire, I thought my suffering was being imposed on me from the outside—the law school needed me to teach; my family couldn't get by unless I got healthy. But now I saw that these were nothing more than stories I'd been telling myself. No one at the law school or in my family had been making those demands on me. *I* was the source of those demands. And even if others had been making demands on me, I realized there was no reason for me to turn their outer critic into my inner critic.

These insights in themselves changed my response to my inner critic because, when I saw the suffering that I was imposing on myself, I thought: "I'm a decent person. I don't deserve this kind of treatment from myself." Then, in a calm and gentle voice, I began to intentionally turn those drill sergeant thoughts around. Initially, this new voice of compassion felt fake, but I persisted, following the instruction for cultivating any sublime state: even if it doesn't feel genuine, do it anyway because so long as your intention is benevolent, you'll be planting a seed. Sure enough, the sentiments gradually became genuine. When that second-person drill sergeant voice shifted to the first person, I took it as a sign that my loyalty had shifted to myself:

"You look like a fool at the law school for not recovering enough to teach" *became* "It's extremely hard to give up a career that I love so much."

"You've ruined your family's life with this stupid illness" *became* "Unexpected things happen in life; I'm in a body and, despite my best efforts, sometimes bodies get sick."

"You *will* get up tomorrow not feeling sick" *became* "My sweet body, working so hard to support me."

Each time I opened my heart to my suffering was a moment of peace because it was a moment of acknowledging my life as it was and engaging it with understanding and compassion. The intention to relieve my suffering grew stronger and stronger, and eventually the inner critic faded away (although it still occasionally pops in for a visit).

I hope you'll try *transforming your inner critic*. Begin by making a list of the self-critical thoughts you've directed at yourself in the past few days or weeks. Take your time. You may not think you remember very many, but they're stored in your brain. Many of us harbor—deep down—a sense of unworthiness, but this is due to past conditioning and we can change how we see ourselves.

As you make your list, leave space between each item. I'll use this self-critical thought as an example: "I can't do anything right."

Look at the first thought you wrote down and imagine that a loved one said that about him- or herself. In other words, imagine if your child or your dearest friend were to say to you, "I can't do anything right." Think about how you would respond to that person and jot it down in the first person. Following my example, under "I can't do anything right" you might write: "It's hard to do everything right, but I'm doing my best." Note that you've just said to yourself what you'd say to a loved one in need of your support.

Go through your list and repeat this process with each self-critical thought you've written down. It's okay if, as you turn the thought around, the new version doesn't feel genuine. Recognize that you're breaking a habit by reconditioning your mind to respond with kindness and compassion, and that this takes time and patience.

If you find yourself thinking, "But I *don't* try hard enough to do things right," or "But I *don't* do my best," treat it as chatter in the mind that comes and goes and need not be believed. Sometimes I keep myself from falling for my self-critical stories by saying lightly to myself, "That's what the mind does—think and emote, think and emote!" In this way, I don't let storytelling dukkha torpedo my efforts to treat myself with compassion.

Keep your list close by. Reading through it every day will remind you to think differently about yourself. You can even add self-critical thoughts to the list as they arise and then turn them around. If your inner critic makes it hard to turn a critical thought into a noncritical one, remember to think about how you'd respond if a loved one had spoken that way about him- or herself. With practice and what Buddhists call patient endurance, *you'll* become that loved one.

Compassion for Sadness Brought About by Loss

All of us have our share of the ten thousand sorrows. Many of them are related to loss—loss of a loved one, loss of a job or career, loss of a home, loss of health, loss of physical or mental functioning due to aging, loss of direction in life, a perceived loss of dignity or usefulness to others. Sometimes life can feel like an endless procession of losses. The sadness that accompanies loss can be so painful to bear that we may fight against letting ourselves feel that sadness by responding in any number of unskillful ways: resignation, anger, solace in sensual indulgences, even anesthetizing ourselves with substance abuse.

We get stuck in these unskillful distractions because we don't want to feel the emotional pain. The skillful response to our sadness would be compassion for ourselves. But compassion cannot arise until we're able to acknowledge that emotional pain is present in the form of sadness. If you sense that you're distracting yourself from feeling the pain of sadness brought about by loss, you might try the four-step approach we've been working with throughout the book: *recognize it, label it, investigate it, let it be.* This can soften your heart and be the beginning of your ability to treat yourself with compassion over the many losses that are an inevitable part of life.

Crafting Compassion Phrases

When I first learned to cultivate compassion, my teachers suggested that we repeat phrases that were nonspecific, such as "May my suffering ease." From years of practice, I've learned that self-compassion practice is more effective if I craft phrases that speak to the particular circumstance over which I'm suffering.

To try this, call to mind some source of suffering for you at this moment. The easiest way to find that place of suffering is to focus on something you want and aren't getting, or on something you're getting and don't want. It could involve your finances, your job, your relationship with certain people, the state of your health, and, of course, sadness and grief due to all the losses I just discussed.

Now speak to yourself about this source of suffering by thinking of compassionate phrases that address your specific situation.

A good way to check if your words show care and compassion is to think about whether you'd say them to a loved one who shared with you that he or she was suffering due to a similar circumstance. It may take time to find the right phrase that speaks to your suffering, but you'll know when you do; it will feel right and may even bring tears to your eyes. But these will be tears of compassion for yourself. In the words of Lord Byron, "The dew of compassion is a tear," and so these tears are likely to leave you feeling relieved and at peace with your circumstances. Your phrases might take this form:

- ► "It's hard to struggle with money every day of my life."
- ► "My job is stressful, but it's not my fault; I'm doing the best I can."
- ► "This relationship is really tough, but I'm working hard at it."
- ► "It hurts that I'm too sick to go to the wedding."
- ► "I'm so sad that, due to aging, I can't do some of my favorite things anymore."

As you say your phrases, you might stroke one arm with the hand of the other. I do this often and find that when my phrases are accompanied by this physical touch, the words penetrate my heart.

Compassion in Action

Treating ourselves with compassion can go beyond using phrases that speak to our suffering. We can also cultivate self-compassion by taking action to alleviate our suffering. Compassionate action can be as simple as pampering ourselves on a day when we're feeling blue or disappointed over something, or it can be as major as leaving a job because we're too sick to continue working.

Compassionate action also includes knowing when not to act—

when to give up a fight that's a continual source of stress and frustration. My friend Michael has decided, for now, to give up his ongoing battle for disability benefits. Despite suffering from a debilitating pain condition, under the laws of his country, he has to apply for benefits each year anew and go through the entire process from square one each time. Some days his pain is so severe that he's not even able to make the trip to see the government caseworker.

When he decided not to reapply for benefits, he felt guilty about it at first. But I thought it was an act of self-compassion. With some budget-tightening, he and his partner can get by on her salary, and she supports his decision to give up the fight for now. With the help of his partner and his friends, he's come to see that the stress and suffering that accompany this annual battle take too great a physical and emotional toll. Yes, he's still upset at the government, but he's decided that self-compassion comes first.

From Self-Compassion to Compassion for Others

If you're still struggling to treat yourself with compassion because you think of it as too self-absorbed, recall the Buddha's words, "If you search the whole world over, you will find no one who is dearer than yourself." In fact, self-compassion can become the seed for being able to reach out to others with compassion because, when we take care of ourselves, we're better able to take care of others.

In the fall of 1992, I learned the hard way that treating myself with compassion was not selfish but, on the contrary, was the key to being able to effectively help others. I had left the comfort of the classroom to become the dean of students at the law school. Student after student came into my office and poured out his or her life troubles to me, partly because I already had the reputation of being approachable as a faculty member.

I thought I owed every student 100 percent of my time and effort, even if it meant skipping lunch or working into the night. Some of them should have been taking their personal problems to the counseling center because I wasn't a trained therapist. This is often where I sent them, but not before listening to them for as long as they wanted. (This work was in addition to the many administrative tasks I'd taken on—supervising the financial aid, placement, and registrar's offices—to name just three.)

After a few months on the job, I was physically exhausted and emotionally spent from trying to give students every ounce of my understanding and compassion. I could tell that I was losing my ability to be effective on the job. Any of you who are caregivers or who work in pastoral care, including hospice, may recognize this phenomenon as compassion burnout. At the time, though, I didn't know this expression, but I did know the Buddha's teachings on suffering, and so that's where I started.

By looking deeply at what was going on in my mind, I saw that I was suffering because of my desire to please everyone, compounded by my fear that I wouldn't be able to do it. I also saw that this suffering was intensified by self-judgment—the feeling that I *should* be able to handle the demands of the job with ease. Until I examined what was going on in my mind, I assumed that the suffering was being imposed on me from the outside. This was the same erroneous assumption I made with the inner critic when I got sick and convinced myself that the demand to get better was coming from others instead of from my own mind.

Having recognized the source of my suffering, I reached out to myself with compassion. I changed my storyline from "I should be able to give everyone 100 percent of my attention all the time" to "This job is really hard; I'm doing the best I can." This change in perspective transformed me into my own ally. I immediately realized that to do my best for the students, I had to take care of myself. And so, I made some changes in the way I performed my duties—self-compassion in action—and this enabled me to more skillfully handle the demands on my time.

By treating myself with compassion, I not only began to enjoy the job but I was able to be a more compassionate presence for the students I was trying to serve. To me, treating ourselves with compassion is just plain good—and practical—common sense.

Using Tonglen to Evoke Compassion for Yourself

The compassion meditation practice known as *tonglen* is generally thought of as a practice for evoking compassion for others, but it's equally as effective for evoking compassion for ourselves. It comes from the Tibetan Buddhist tradition. Tonglen is practiced on the in- and on the out-breath. The general instruction is to breathe in the suffering of others and then, as we breathe out, release that suffering and offer to them whatever measure of kindness, compassion, and peace of mind we have to give, even the slightest bit. We are, in effect, breathing out the sublime states of mind.

I practice tonglen when I become aware that I'm suffering due to something in particular, like my inability to attend an event due to poor health. I bring to mind all the people who might be suffering in the same way I am. Then I breathe in their suffering. As I do this, I'm aware that, because I share the same struggle with the people whom I've brought to mind, I'm also breathing in my own suffering over that struggle. As I then breathe out whatever measure of kindness, compassion, and peace of mind I have to give at the moment, I'm also offering those sentiments to myself.

Tonglen practice helped me through a particularly difficult period after illness forced me to give up my career. When I left the lively, stimulating environment of the law school and took up residence in my bedroom, I began to suffer from deep loneliness.

Loneliness is a painful emotional state, often accompanied by sadness, rejection, and self-blame. I'm using it as an example because it's not uncommon for people to feel lonely. Even those who work around others all day can have loneliness descend on them when they get home—or even experience it while with others.

Spending most of the day alone in my bedroom, I came to regard loneliness as an enemy. I mustered all the willpower I could to defeat it, but the battle I was waging only created double suffering for me: aversion dukkha and storytelling dukkha. Recall that aversion dukkha arises when we resist the way things are, instead of openly acknowledging the unpleasantness of an experience. I was resisting that loneliness with all my might. Then I was adding storytelling dukkha to the mix in the form of stressful thoughts that had no basis in fact, such as: "This dark feeling will never lift"; "No one cares that I'm by myself so much"; "I'm a weak person because I can't handle being alone."

Although I'd used tonglen many times, it didn't occur to me to try it with the suffering of loneliness until I read a blog post one day. It was written by a woman who was chronically ill and was also suffering from terrible loneliness. Her story resonated strongly with me because she was describing just how I felt. Wanting to reach out to her in some way, I imagined breathing in her suffering due to the loneliness. Then, as I breathed out, I genuinely wished that her suffering would ease. To my surprise, *my own* suffering eased.

I continued with the practice, at first using it only with this woman. Eventually, I expanded it to include everyone in the world who was lonely. Tonglen became a powerful self-compassion practice for easing my suffering. Whenever I called to mind the millions of people who were feeling lonely like I was, I felt a deep connection to them. That connection in itself made me feel less lonely. In addition, whenever I breathed out whatever kindness, compassion, and peace of mind I had to offer them, I was also breathing those sentiments into my own heart. I found myself saying: "It's okay to be lonely. Yes, it's painful, but it will change and isn't a permanent part of me."

I encourage you to try tonglen. You can practice it in regard to something that's an ongoing source of suffering for you, like loneliness or chronic worrying. Or you can practice it when something short term is causing you stress or anxiety, like waiting to hear the results of a medical test or of a job interview. For example, if you just interviewed for a job, you could breathe in the suffering and anxiety of everyone who is waiting to find out the results of an interview, and then breathe out whatever kindness, compassion, and peace of mind you have to offer—to them and to yourself.

If you find it difficult to breathe in other people's suffering, then modify the practice. Rather than taking in their suffering on the in-breath, just breathe normally and call to mind the people with whom you wish to connect. Then, in whatever way feels natural to you, send them thoughts of kindness, compassion, and peace. You need not breathe in others' suffering in order to feel connected to them or in order to enfold both them and yourself in your heartfelt wish to ease suffering in this world.

It may take time to learn to treat yourself with compassion because you may be reversing a lifetime of conditioning. Many of us have been taught that nothing less than perfection will do. This may have been instilled in us by our parents or other influential people in our lives (people who are, of course, imperfect just like us). As a result, we hold ourselves to impossible standards; we're the Beatles or we're nothing.

If this is the case for you, you may initially resist treating yourself with compassion or, when you do try to cultivate it, feel sadness arise. This sadness may well be due to a realization that this is the first time in your life you've truly treated yourself kindly. Think of it, then, as a sweet sadness. The Dalai Lama repeatedly reminds us that everyone wants to be happy. "Everyone" includes you—this person most worthy of your kindness and compassion. With practice, self-compassion can become a natural response to your suffering.

17

Appreciative Joy: An Antidote to Envy and Resentment

Whenever you hear that someone else has been successful,
rejoice. Always practice rejoicing for others—whether your
friend or your enemy. If you cannot practice rejoicing,
no matter how long you live, you will not be happy.

—LAMA ZOPA RINPOCHE

IN THE EARLIER discussion of the sublime state of appreciative joy, recall how, when Octavia Spencer won an Oscar, Tony and I spontaneously delighted in her joy as we watched her pick up her award. My happiness for her was genuine, but it didn't present an appreciative joy challenge for me. As I watched her, I wasn't thinking: "That's not fair. *I* should have won that Oscar!" But what if I were an actress nominated in the same category? Would envy and perhaps even resentment have hindered my ability to feel joy for her? Quite possibly!

Appreciative joy practice deepens when we're able to feel genuine joy for someone in a situation that could easily give rise to envy and resentment. Envy is present when we're unhappy and discontented because of someone else's possessions, traits, accomplishments, or even plain good luck. Resentment accompanies envy when we also feel bitter because we believe we've been treated unfairly by that person or by the world. Resentment is a form of the second hindrance—anger or ill-will.

Here's an example of envy: "*I* want a new car like the one my neighbor just got." Here's an example of envy accompanied by resentment: "I want that car and it's not fair that he got it and I didn't. I work just as hard as he does." If you noticed the word *want* in both of those examples, it's because both envy and resentment have their source in the self-focused desire that characterizes tanha. With envy, we want what someone else has. And if we believe we're not getting it because of some perceived unfairness or injustice, then resentment is present too.

Working with Envy and Resentment

Once you've familiarized yourself with cultivating appreciative joy by practicing with people for whom it's easy for you to feel joy—a child having fun, a loved one laughing, someone on an award show—I encourage you to go a step further by thinking of someone toward whom you're feeling envy, or both envy and resentment.

Here are some examples of what might give rise to envy and resentment in your life: a friend in a new romantic relationship; a former coworker who's landed a more desirable job; a friend who's in great physical shape; family members who can afford to take fancy vacations; friends who don't have caregiver responsibilities; an acquaintance who doesn't seem to have a care in the world.

Try not to judge yourself negatively for feeling envy or resentment. After all, I imagine everyone feels it some time during his or her life. If you feel judgment start to arise, remember to be compassionate toward yourself, using whatever words speak to your suffering, such as "It's hard to keep envy from arising when I want what she has, but I'm going to work on being happy for her."

With self-compassion at your side, call to mind the person whom you've chosen to work with. Imagine him or her in the joyful situation that's the source of your envy (or your envy and resentment). Try to appreciate this person's happiness even a little. If you can't, with your wisdom mind, reflect on how envy and resentment are mental states that reflect a desire to have life conform to your liking, but how it's simply impossible to always get what you want. Then try again.

This time, silently speak a phrase that directly touches this person's joy, such as "May your new relationship continue to make you happy"; "May your new job continue to be satisfying to you"; "May you enjoy your vacation." Speaking phrases like this can help loosen the grip of envy and resentment because the words take us out of our self-focused thinking and open our hearts to another person's experience.

Responding with appreciative joy—as would an awakened being—takes practice and patience, but when we're able to be happy for others in the face of envy and resentment, both of them gradually fade away. In this way, appreciative joy becomes a liberation practice because it frees us from the suffering that accompanies these two painful mental states.

By way of example, here's how I worked with envy and resentment when they arose for two people whom I love dearly. In the summer of 2011, Tony and our granddaughter Malia travelled from California to New York City for a week's vacation. Due to my health limitations, I wasn't able to go. I thought I was in good shape with my appreciative joy practice, that is, until I began getting text messages and emailed pictures from New York. Instead of feeling happy for them, I felt sad and even irritated.

Because I had wanted them to go on this trip—indeed, I'd encouraged them and had helped plan it—I was confused by my reaction. I'd expected to rejoice in their joy every time I heard from them. Because this wasn't happening, I began to judge myself negatively: "Why aren't you thrilled for them? How selfish." Oh, that inner critic—always waiting in the wings.

Looking at what was going on in my mind, it finally dawned on me. I was envious of them! At first, I said, "No, that can't be." But there it was: envy. I wanted what they had. And behind the envy was a feeling that it wasn't fair that they were there without me. So there was some resentment present too—not against them, personally, but against a world that was so unjust as to make it impossible for me to travel.

When I finally recognized that envy and resentment were behind my sadness and irritation and self-criticism, compassion for myself almost instantly arose. I've thought about why compassion jumped right in and pushed that inner critic aside. I think it was because I was so utterly surprised to discover I was feeling envy and resentment about this trip that I'd wanted them so badly to take, that my heart just broke open with compassion for the suffering I was experiencing. I found myself saying: "Wow. I had no idea that this trip of theirs would be painful for me; life can sure be hard sometimes."

With compassion for my sadness as my companion—along with my uninvited but tolerated guests, envy and resentment—I turned to the cultivation of appreciative joy. It was hard at first. I would visualize them on their outings—chatting with each other, smiling and laughing. The Staten Island Ferry. The Empire State Building. The Guggenheim Museum. The transformation was slow, but gradually my heart opened to the good time they were having, and the envy and resentment gave way to a feeling of joy for their happiness. By the end of the trip, I was not only happy for them, I felt as if they were in New York *for* me, and so I felt joy for myself as well.

Deepening the Practice

You can deepen your practice even further by cultivating appreciative joy for people you don't like. I pick politicians whose views are the polar opposite of mine. The joyful occasion I use to practice appreciative joy is an election victory for them. It can be a challenge just to cultivate metta—friendliness—toward them, so feeling appreciative joy for their good fortune can definitely show me my limits! But I know that resenting them for winning only makes me suffer.

As I watch them on television, rejoicing with their families, I reflect on how they are human beings like me and how we share the same hopes and dreams for our loved ones. We just have different views on what will bring about the happiness and well-being we seek. This reflection helps me to feel joy for them, even in the midst of my disappointment over the election results. I've come to realize that I can feel both disappointment *and* appreciative joy— disappointment over my chosen candidate's loss and joy for the other candidate's delight in his or her victory. It may not lessen my resolve to help defeat this person when re-election time rolls around, but it lessens my suffering over not having gotten what I wanted.

Practicing appreciative joy in the face of envy and resentment is an ongoing challenge for me. Despite over twenty years of Buddhist practice, invariably, when Tony leaves for Berkeley or Los Angeles to spend time with one of our granddaughters, envy and sometimes resentment arise. But as soon as I become mindful that they've arisen, I greet them as old (if not favorite) guests.

Then I reflect on how envy has arisen because Tony is getting what I myself want, but that it's a want that, given my health, just can't be satisfied. I also reflect on how resentment over my health—

the conviction that I've been done an injustice by the world—is delusional. My wisdom mind knows that, having been born, I'm subject to bodily difficulties. It happens differently for each person. This is how it's happening to me. I also reflect on how unhappy envy and resentment make me feel, and how neither one of them gets me any closer to Berkeley or Los Angeles.

Then I turn my attention to appreciative joy. I begin to cultivate joy for them, picturing what a wonderful time they'll be having together. Eventually, a soothing and healing feeling of happiness for them arises, and the suffering from my desire to be with them gives way to a feeling of peace with my life as it is.

I hope you'll practice "rejoicing for others," as Lama Zopa Rinpoche calls it in the quotation that begins this chapter. Cultivating appreciative joy may be a challenge at times but, with practice, it will open your heart and fill it with joy.

18

Equanimity:
Fully Engaging This Life as It Is

If you expect your life to be up and down,
your mind will be much more peaceful.

—LAMA YESHE

A MIND THAT is equanimous responds to life with an evenness of temper and a peaceful heart, even when the circumstances at hand may be one of those ten thousand sorrows—tension in a relationship, anxiety over children or parents, stress at work or at school, health difficulties, loss of a loved one. Every moment of equanimity is a moment of waking up from the delusion that things should be as we want them to be.

When we learn not to reject unpleasant experiences, we're able to make room for the sorrow in our hearts and, treating it tenderly, rest in the peace and ease of equanimity. In the same way, when we learn not to cling to pleasant experiences—the ten thousand joys in our lives—we're acknowledging that we cannot make the impermanent permanent. Then, resting in equanimity, we can enjoy the experience while it lasts.

The sublime states are usually presented in the sequence found in Chapter Thirteen: kindness and friendliness, compassion, appreciative joy, and equanimity. But in her book *It's Easier Than You Think*, Sylvia Boorstein starts with equanimity. She says that from the place of equanimity—holding both our joys and sorrows "in an ease-filled balance"—when we see people going about their everyday lives, friendliness is our natural response. When we see someone suffering, compassion is our natural response. When we see someone who's happy, appreciative joy is our natural response.

One evening in February of 2012, I had an experience that brought into clear focus what it means to hold both our joys and sorrows in an ease-filled balance. The wispy clouds in the western sky were setting up for a spectacular sunset. I saw the sunset forming from my living room window, so I went outside and sat on the porch to watch. Unaware that Tony had turned on network news, I became absorbed in the beauty of the display before me. Suddenly, Tony appeared at my side, saying in a troubled voice: "The Syrian government is shooting civilians in the streets. People are running out of food and water." (He was as absorbed in this news story as I was in the sunset, and so he was unaware that he was interrupting my pleasant experience.)

My first thought was, "You shouldn't break in on my joyful moment like this." Then I veered in the other direction and thought, "I shouldn't be enjoying this sunset when people are dying in Syria." Within a few seconds, I'd judged him and then judged myself. I felt caught in a dilemma: "What do I do about this unpleasant experience colliding with this pleasant one?" Then equanimity came to mind, and I thought: "This sunset is beautiful *and* people are dying in Syria. I need not cling to joy to the exclusion of all other experiences, and I need not recoil from sorrow. My heart is big enough to hold the joy of this sunset and, at the same time, the suffering of the Syrian people." And so I sat there and tenderly held them both in an ease-filled balance.

Let's consider some skillful means for cultivating equanimity.

"Start Where You Are"

Recall that dukkha refers to the dissatisfaction we experience with the circumstances of our lives. This dissatisfaction has its source in the type of desire that's experienced as a felt-need for our lives to be different, even when we have no control over the circumstances in question.

After becoming chronically ill in 2001, I spent my days caught up in constant longing for my life to be the way it was before I got sick. I wanted to work. I wanted to travel. I wanted to be active in the life of my family and my community. But no amount of wishing for my circumstances to be different got me any closer to resuming my former life. Finally, I realized the only way I could find a measure of peace again was to stop trying to change circumstances over which I had no control and instead—to reference Pema Chödrön again—*start where I was*, with a body that was sick. For you, starting where you are might mean acknowledging frustration on the job, or disappointment with a relationship, or the stress of being a caregiver.

Remember not to confuse the calm acceptance of equanimity with resignation or indifference. The latter two are characterized by aversion to life, meaning we're turning away from the way things are. When we turn away, it's hard to make constructive changes because we're not engaging with our life as it is. By contrast, when we *start where we are*, we're better able to consider what might be the most skillful and beneficial action given our circumstances. For me, this means remaining proactive about my health. Returning to my examples, for you, it might mean keeping an eye out for a new job, or suggesting that you and your partner consider couples therapy, or looking for ways to get help with your caregiving responsibilities.

I hope you'll resolve to *start where you are* each day. When you get up in the morning, if your struggles are the first thing that pop into your mind, reflect on how everyone's life is sometimes easy and sometimes hard. No one gets a pass on life's struggles. If you can acknowledge the difficulties you're facing, you'll be less likely to get caught up in longing for circumstances over which you have no control to be different. And you'll be more likely to see clearly whether there's any constructive action you could take to improve those circumstances that you *can* affect. In this way, you can be present for your life as it is for you on this day and, no matter what your difficulties, find some measure of peace and well-being.

Accepting and engaging my life as it is, difficulties and disappointments included, is a daily practice and I fall short at times. In 2011, my friend Grazia was in an auto accident that almost took her life. When I visited her after she was home from the hospital, to lighten the mood, we joked that although right now she was worse off than I was, in a few months she'd be better off again. Sure enough, she's recovered enough to resume her active life.

At the time of her recovery, I thought back to when she was in a neck brace and in severe pain and how, now, she was traveling all over the world but I was still mostly housebound. The thought arose, "This isn't fair." Thoughts pop into my mind uninvited all the time, so I didn't blame myself for this self-focused one. But I also knew that "This isn't fair" was not the response of a mind that is at peace. So I reflected on Grazia's life and on mine and said to myself: "This is the way our lives are—it's that way for her and this way for me." Then I rejoiced in her recovery and got on with my day as it was.

Buddhist monks carry a bowl for food and eat only what is put into that bowl each day. A bowl may be filled to the top with mouth-watering food or it may contain a small handful of rice. This is how monks are taught to *start where they are*. The monk's bowl can be seen as a metaphor for life. We have what is put into our individual bowls each day. It's up to us to learn to accept and engage it with grace.

Let Impermanence Be Your Guide

If you're like me, some days you feel cheerful and optimistic about everything, and other days you feel in low spirits—often for no discernable reason. When we're feeling dispirited, recognizing the ever-changing nature of experience can keep us from believing that we're permanently trapped in a dark mood. In the same way, when we're feeling ecstatic about life, understanding impermanence can keep us from clinging to this feeling which only sets us up for suffering—and perhaps a wild mood-swing in the other direction—when that euphoria goes away. And so cultivating wisdom—in this instance, looking deeply at impermanence—helps us to maintain the steadiness of mind and the evenness of temper that characterize equanimity.

Understanding the impermanent nature of all phenomena also helps us recognize that we are more than our emotions and moods. This is particularly helpful when our spirits are low. When we see clearly that we are *not* just sadness or that we are *not* just irritation, we're better able to calmly wait, with equanimity, for things to change.

I think of emotions and moods as being as changeable and unpredictable as the weather. They blow in; they blow out. By working with this weather metaphor, we can hold these mental states more lightly—with the evenness of temper that characterizes equanimity—knowing that, like the weather pattern of the moment, our emotions and moods are impermanent. It's also helpful to think of emotions and moods as being like the ever-changing waves on the ocean. Keeping this comparison in mind, we can work on calmly and steadily riding life's ups and downs like the most skilled of surfers.

If You Can't Change It, Let It Be

If you find yourself in circumstances you cannot change, I hope you'll try a practice I call *if you can't change it, let it be*. When my book *How to Be Sick* was released, I had the opportunity to work with this practice. At the time, the largest bookstore in my town was a Borders—and it didn't carry my book. Invariably, my first thought upon entering the store was a grumpy "Borders doesn't carry my book" (as if I didn't know this already!).

Then my list of complaints would begin:

- ► "There are tens of thousands of books here. Why not mine? This is so unfair!"
- ► "What an incompetent bunch of buyers to have passed on my book. No wonder they're going out of business." (Note the self-centered delusion in *that* statement: Borders was in financial trouble because it failed to carry my book!)
- ► "Maybe I should talk to the manager. He could call corporate headquarters and tell them they've made a big mistake!"

It was my own exquisite little scene of torture and I replayed it every time I went into the store. Then one day, I recalled a daylong retreat I'd attended with the Thai Buddhist monk Ajahn Jumnian. At one point, he had begun to describe how he lived each day. As

Jack Kornfield translated, I grabbed pen and paper and jotted this down:

> When people say, "Ajahn, let's go for a beautiful walk," fine I'll go. If they don't ask, that's fine too. I don't expect a walk to be any more satisfying than sitting alone. It could be hot or windy out there. If people bring me delicious food, great. If they don't, great. I need to diet anyway. If I'm feeling good, that's okay. If I'm sick, that's okay too. It's a great excuse to lie down.

I had this little discourse memorized, so I decided to use it as inspiration the next time I entered the store. When the day came, as soon as I started to list my complaints, I stopped and said to myself: "If Borders carried my book, fine. Since it's not here, fine. It gives me the opportunity to practice equanimity—letting be what I cannot change." Then I began to cultivate mindfulness by turning my attention to what was going on around me at that moment. It was a beautiful sight: people calmly meandering down rows of books; someone excitedly motioning for a friend to come over so she could share some treasure she'd found; a young girl, sitting on the floor, completely absorbed in the pages of an art book. I felt a sudden affection for this bookstore. In that moment, it didn't matter at all that my book wasn't in it!

I hope you'll try practicing *if you can't change it, let it be*. I suggest that you start with a minor irritation like those I raised in the equanimity portion of Chapter Thirteen: a loud restaurant or a day that's too hot for your liking. By practicing with mildly unpleasant experiences, we're training our minds to respond with an evenness of temper and a peaceful heart when we're faced with a life crisis, such as being rejected by another person, receiving an upsetting medical diagnosis, or even the loss of a loved one. So start small.

Try thinking about someone who has a behavioral trait that irritates you—nothing major—perhaps a whiny relative, or a complaining friend, or a coworker who asks too many questions. Recalling Ajahn Jumnian's words, say to yourself something like: "If this person's behavior changes, that would be nice. If it doesn't change, that will be okay too."

How did you react when you said your words? With a loud "No it won't be okay!"? If so, reflect on how your life will inevitably be a mixture of pleasant and unpleasant experiences. This person's behavior is an example of an experience that is unpleasant for you. Turning away in aversion only increases your suffering by adding the unpleasantness of aversion to an *already* unpleasant experience. You might also reflect on my twist on Walt Whitman's verse and say to yourself: "*The world contains multitudes . . .* and so it's big enough for people who irritate me." Then bring to mind the person you were thinking of and try the practice again.

A bigger challenge is to apply Ajahn Jumnian's words to sensitive issues about yourself—for example, how much you weigh or certain habits or traits that you wish were different. You might try bringing one of those issues to mind and then speaking to yourself from Ajahn Jumnian's perspective: "If I'm able to lose weight, fine. If I can't, that will be okay too"; "If I can learn to be more assertive around others, that will be nice. If I'm unable to, I can accept that." When we're able to accept ourselves as we are, we've shed yet another layer of suffering.

I feel confident that, with practice, you can begin to experience the feeling of peace and well-being that comes from letting be what you cannot change, even when you're confronted with the toughest of life's challenges. Letting be what you cannot change is not to be confused with indifference to your life as it is. Indifference carries aversion with it, and so the suffering of *don't-want* is present: "Well, whatever. Who cares?" A mind that is equanimous knows that life is a mixture of successes and disappointments and that peace of mind comes from acknowledging this with grace and acceptance, not from turning away in aversion.

Develop an Assumption of Safety

When I got sick, Sylvia Boorstein gave me a book called *Healing Lazarus* by Zen teacher Lewis Richmond. In the prime of his life, Richmond was struck down with a rare life-threatening brain injury—viral encephalitis. He was in a coma for ten days. In this remarkable book, he chronicles the devastating effect of the illness and his slow climb back to health.

One story he told had a profound effect on me. When he began to recover, he had to put his life back together. This meant learning how to walk and talk, resuming his career, and becoming an equal partner in his family life. During this long and grueling process, he suddenly found himself living in overwhelming fear and worry that something like this illness could happen to him again.

His therapist identified this fear as a phenomenon called "catastrophic thinking." She told him that this was not unusual to experience after a traumatic event. Then she said:

> Of course, any of those things might happen, to you or to me or to anyone, but we can't live our lives in fear of them. We all must develop an assumption of safety that allows us to get through the day. I have three children, and if I allowed myself to worry constantly that one of them might be hit by a car, or could be kidnapped, I wouldn't be able to function.

These words from his therapist have helped me cultivate that evenness of temper and ease-filled balance of equanimity. I can still get caught up in the fear generated by uncertainty: "What if one of my children or grandchildren is at a shopping mall when a terrorist attack occurs?"; "What if someone in my family is in a bad auto accident?"—the latter being a fear I've carried since childhood. But now, when these fears arise, I remember what Richmond's therapist told him and I repeat her words to myself: "We all must develop an assumption of safety."

This comment of hers has not only helped me cope with the uncertainty of being chronically ill, but I've also relaxed about my children and grandchildren. I've wrapped them in an assumption of safety. It's been tremendously comforting and freeing for me. After all, the probability is low that anything disastrous will happen to them. Of course we should take reasonable precautions, but catastrophes are the exception not the rule, despite the media's constant focus on them. Yes, something terrible could happen. We all know that. But the assumption of safety, accompanied by reasonable precautions, is the skillful alternative to living in worry and fear every time you or your loved ones leave the house.

You might try practicing with the *assumption of safety* by calling to mind one of your own recurring worries or fears, something that keeps you from feeling the peace and calmness that characterize equanimity. As you do this, remind yourself that worry and fear are just arising and passing emotions—and that the stressful stories accompanying them also arise and pass. Neither the emotions nor the stories you spin have any connection to whether or not the subject of your worry and fear will ever come to pass. With that in mind, allow yourself to develop an assumption of safety about that fear or worry. It might help to recall what Mark Twain famously said: "I've lived a long life and seen a lot of hard times . . . most of which never happened."

Loving Your Fate

It takes courage to accept and engage your life as it is. Frederick Nietzsche called this *amor fati*—loving your fate. In those moments when you're able to muster the courage to let your heart break wide open to embrace all of your life as it is, you're loving your fate. The Thai Buddhist monk Ajahn Chah called this "the happiness of the Buddha." I've been calling it awakening—waking up to a peace and well-being that aren't dependent on whether a particular moment is pleasant or unpleasant.

I'm quite certain that you won't get through this day without encountering some unpleasant experience, whether it be your computer crashing, being put on hold for a very long time, stubbing your toe, forgetting what you headed into the kitchen to retrieve, or feeling terribly disappointed by someone. When this happens, I encourage you to practice *loving your fate*.

Loving your fate doesn't mean you shouldn't take action to improve things personally and globally when that action can lessen suffering for you and for others. It simply means that your starting point is *life as it is*. Loving your fate means working to accept, with grace, that life will be a mixture of ten thousand joys and ten thousand sorrows, and opening your heart regardless.

This can be quite a challenge. I didn't love my fate when I first lost my career. And I still struggle to love my fate when I think about my inability to spend long periods of time with my two grand-daughters, Malia and Camden. Malia lives in Los Angeles—the city where I grew up—so I thought I'd be showing her all my secret haunts. And Cam lives in Berkeley, right across the bridge from San Francisco, a city that I dearly love. I'd hoped to take her to all my favorite places: Fort Point, Aquatic Park, Fisherman's Wharf.

As you can tell, this particular struggle is an ongoing equanimity challenge for me. Recall that the Buddha said that what we repeatedly think and ponder upon becomes the inclination of our minds. And so, I know that every time I respond with bitterness over my inability to be with my granddaughters—that is, every time I hate my fate—I strengthen my tendency to respond that way again. So I work on loving my fate.

I start with equanimity—reflecting on the wisdom of letting be what I cannot change. Then I move in a circle through the other three sublime states and, finally, back to equanimity. I cultivate appreciative joy for Malia's and Cam's other grandparents who *are* able to take them places. I cultivate kindness for myself and compassion for the suffering I experience at *not* being able to. Then I return to equanimity by reflecting on how everyone's life has its joys and sorrows. If I could be with them more, I would, but since I can't, I work on loving my fate regardless—a fate which has me living in a comfortable home, with a loving partner, a supportive family, a few good friends, and a faithful hound dog.

When we're able to engage our lives without clinging to joy and without turning away from sorrow, then we're touching that evenness of temper and openness of heart that characterize equanimity. In those moments, we feel alive to our experience as it is, whether it's pleasant or unpleasant, whether it's to our liking or not.

This is the promise of peace that the Buddha said is possible for all of us to attain.

19

Intentionally Turning Your Mind to the Sublime States

*The greatest weapon against stress is our ability
to choose one thought over another.*

—WILLIAM JAMES

SOME YEARS AGO, a birthday party for my granddaughter Camden provided the setting for a powerful experience along the Buddha's path. In the midst of a painful bout of suffering, I was able to change course by intentionally turning my mind to the cultivation of the four sublime states. In other words, I was able to choose to engage my experience as would an awakened being.

The birthday party took place at a park near my son and daughter-in-law's house, which is over an hour from where I live. It started at 10:30 in the morning. Factoring in my need to nap in the early afternoon due to illness and, given the round-trip driving time (even with someone else driving), I knew I couldn't stay for the whole party. Still, I decided to push myself and go for about an hour and a half.

When I got there, I was happy and content. Yes, I couldn't stay for the entire party but here I was with Camden, her little friends and their parents, my daughter-in-law's parents and her brother, and even an old friend who was there with her granddaughter.

At one point, I asked my son Jamal if his best friends were coming—a couple I dearly love but rarely get to see. He said apologetically (knowing I wouldn't be able to attend) that they were coming over to his house along with other friends for the "adult party" that evening. Whoa! That contentment disappeared in a flash. My desire to go to the evening party was so overwhelming, I could feel the muscles in my body tightening and my face getting flushed. Then envy and resentment reared their unpleasant heads, and I began spinning stressful stories like: "This isn't fair because Camden's other grandparents get to go"; "Everyone will be talking and eating and laughing without me"; "Tonight is when the *real* fun will start."

Not wanting others to see how I felt, I took myself off to the restroom to regroup (you could say I gave myself a time-out). Was I going to let this information ruin the rest of my time at the party? I didn't want it to, but envy and resentment and the storytelling dukkha that accompanied them had driven away all the happiness and contentment I'd been feeling.

I knew that the source of my suffering and dissatisfaction was my desire to go to the party that evening—a desire so intense that it felt as if my happiness and contentment were dependent on fulfilling it. I also knew that my misery was being compounded by the envy and resentment I was feeling toward others who would be there. But beyond these insights, I felt stuck.

When I'm stuck, I always look more deeply at the Buddha's teachings on suffering because he repeatedly said that he taught dukkha and the end of dukkha. As I investigated my suffering, I saw that it was being intensified by the strong aversion I was feeling toward what was happening. I *didn't want* to be driven by desire. I *didn't want* to be feeling envy and resentment. This is the *don't-want* side of desire.

The aversion was taking the form of blaming myself for the presence of these painful mental states. And where there's negative self-judgment, there's more storytelling dukkha. Mine took a form that's embarrassing to relate: "You're a bad Buddhist. All these years of practice and you can't control your mind at all."

Recall the passage I cited in Chapter Ten from Bhante Gunaratana's *Mindfulness in Plain English*: "Your mind is a shrieking, gibbering madhouse on wheels barreling pell-mell down the hill, utterly out of control and hopeless." I certainly could have benefitted from having those words before me, especially his next sentence: "No problem." It would have put what I was feeling into perspective and provided some solace. But I didn't have his book with me. All I had was my body and mind in a dark, dank cement restroom stall that looked not unlike a prison cell. This was fitting because, although my body wasn't in prison, my mind surely was.

After some time, I finally realized that I could keep feeding these painful mental states by going over and over my complaints—not being able to go to the party, not being able to control my mind— or I could acknowledge what I was feeling. And so, I took a deep breath and decided to stop resisting the presence of these painful mental states. I whispered several times: "Desire is present. Envy and resentment are present. Even self-blame is present. It's okay. Just let them be." Those words alone, "let them be," allowed a little light to enter the prison cell of my mind and began to ease my suffering.

As my suffering eased, I realized that I could choose to turn my attention to the cultivation of the four sublime states. I began with compassion. I reached out to my suffering by gently whispering, "It's hard to have to skip a party that I want to go to so badly."

Immediately, I could feel the suffering of desire, envy, and resentment weakening further. Then I even managed a slight smile as I thought: "What's with this bad Buddhist/good Buddhist stuff? Jack Kornfield is right—the mind *has* no shame!" And with that, the self-blame slipped away.

Having started with compassion, I was on a roll and so I began to cultivate the kindness and friendliness that characterize metta. In this instance, I was the one in need of those sentiments, so I said softly, "May I be happy hanging out with my family and the party guests for the rest of my time here."

My heart having been softened by compassion, kindness, and friendliness for myself, I turned my attention to appreciative joy. I began by thinking about the love I feel for Jamal and for my daughter-in-law Bridgett and her family, and I let that love fill my heart. Then I pictured them together that evening, along with other friends, enjoying each other's company. As I did this, I tried to feel joy for the good time they'd be having. It took awhile—the resentment was gone but, at first, the residue of envy was still there. But I kept at it, visualizing even more strongly the good time they'd be having. Eventually, appreciative joy arose for their ability to gather together even though I couldn't be there.

Finally, I was ready to leave my little restroom cell. As I walked back to the party, equanimity arose. I felt content with my life as it was. "Yes, my body is sick and that limits what I can do," I thought, "but this is how my life is and I'm at peace with its joys and its sorrows." I rejoined the party and thoroughly enjoyed the rest of my time there.

Intentionally Turning Your Mind

I encourage you to try this practice of making an intentional choice to turn your mind to cultivating the sublime states. Recall an occa-

sion when you were sad and unhappy because you couldn't participate fully—or at all. Maybe you had work obligations that forced
you either to miss the occasion or to leave early. Maybe financial
constraints kept you from traveling to the event. Maybe health difficulties limited your ability to fully participate. It might have been
a wedding, a holiday party, a school reunion, or a nature outing
with friends.

Pick an event that's still a source of disappointment and sorrow
for you. This occasion will be the subject of this exercise. I have
two recent occasions to call upon. One was the thirtieth reunion
for my law school class; I was too sick to attend. The other was
the wedding of my dear friends Nhi and Greg; I was able to attend
the ceremony, but couldn't stay for the banquet and party that
followed.

Make the memory of the event you've chosen as vivid as you
can, including all the stressful stories you told yourself about it. If
you couldn't go at all, those stories might have taken this form: "It
wasn't fair that I had to miss the backpack trip." If you had to leave
early, your stories might have sounded like this: "I just know that
the *real* fun started after I left the party." To help keep them vivid
in your mind, maybe jot these stories down.

Now begin to explore if you could have eased your suffering had
you intentionally turned your mind to the sublime states. You can
practice with all four, as follows, or pick any number of them to
work with.

Compassion. Consider how you might have evoked compassion
for yourself regarding this occasion. Choose phrases that would
have spoken directly to your suffering. To help you with this exercise, I'll use those two occasions from my own life as examples: the
missed reunion and the partially-attended wedding. My phrases
would have been along these lines: "It's so hard to be missing the

reunion of my very own classmates"; "It hurts to have to leave the wedding early—I feel as if I'm going to miss the best part." If your own compassion phrases bring tears to your eyes, that's fine. They're tears of compassion for your suffering.

Kindness and friendliness. Think about how you could have spoken to yourself with kindness and friendliness about the occasion, despite your disappointment. To help with this, think about what you might have said to a friend who was in that situation and then turn those words into the first person.

I would have told a friend who had to miss a milestone reunion to be especially kind and gentle with herself about it. It wasn't her fault; she'd go if she could. I would have told a friend who couldn't stay for an entire wedding celebration that my heartfelt wish for him was that he be able to enjoy the part of the event that he *was* able to attend.

If I'd then turned these phrases into the first person, I'd have addressed myself in this fashion: "May I be kind and gentle to myself over my inability to attend the reunion"; "Let me enjoy myself as best I can at the wedding, even though I have to leave early."

Appreciative joy. Recall some of the people who were enjoying themselves at your chosen occasion. If you weren't there, try to imagine their joy. If envy and resentment arise, that's okay. Simply acknowledge that they've arisen; then let them be and continue to try and evoke appreciative joy. If you're not able to feel joy for others and begin to judge yourself negatively over it, immediately switch to compassion practice, saying something like: "I'm trying my best to rejoice in their joy, but right now it's just too hard." Feeling joy for others can be a challenge and may not be possible to do at times. That's fine. There are three other sublime states you can work on!

Equanimity. Look back on the occasion and try to see it as one of those *if you can't change it, let it be* moments from the previous chapter. Doing that might help you accept how it was for you. You could use phrases like these: "If I could have gone to the reunion, that would have been nice. But people can't always go to events, even if they badly want to. It's okay." "If I could have stayed for the whole wedding, that would have been a treat. However, I had no choice but to leave early; it's just the way life is for me right now."

Cultivating wisdom can also help us evoke equanimity when we're sad and disappointed about an occasion. For example, when we understand with our wisdom mind that not always getting what we want is a universal human experience, it's easier to accept, with grace, how these events unfolded for us. Equanimity is the ability to open our hearts and minds to our experience as it happened even if it didn't live up to our hopes and expectations. In this vein, I'm inspired by Joseph's Campbell's comment:

> We must let go of the life we have planned, so as to accept
> the one that is waiting for us.

I refer to the sublime states as the psychological states of awakened beings because I've found that when I respond to my experience with kindness and friendliness, compassion, appreciative joy, and equanimity, I'm able to touch the peace that comes with freedom from suffering—the very promise that the Buddha held out for us when he said he taught the cessation of suffering.

I hope you'll explore for yourself and see if, when you're cultivating the sublime states, you feel some of that same peace. These are moments of awakening that come from engaging life with our full potential as caring and compassionate human beings.

In the End . . .

20

Onward Down the Path

Abandon what is unskillful. One can abandon what is
unskillful. If it were not possible, I would not ask you
to do it . . . But as it brings benefit and contentment,
therefore I say, abandon what is unskillful . . .
Cultivate what is skillful. One can cultivate what is
skillful. If it were not possible, I would not ask you
to do it . . . But as this cultivation brings benefit
and contentment, I say cultivate what is skillful.

—THE BUDDHA

THESE WORDS from the Buddha summarize my purpose in writing this book. Following the path he laid out for us, I've tried to point the way to *abandoning what is unskillful*. This includes abandoning the delusion that we can fashion all of our experience to our liking and, in doing so, avoid life's inevitable sorrows. It also includes abandoning the delusion that fulfilling the self-focused desires that drive so much of our behavior will bring sustained and lasting happiness. The Buddha said that abandoning what is unskillful *brings benefit and contentment*.

I've also tried to point the way to *cultivating what is skillful*. This includes understanding suffering and the sources of suffering so that we can act to alleviate it in ourselves and others. Cultivating what is skillful also includes practicing mindfulness so that we become adept at engaging every moment as it is, without clinging to pleasant experiences or rejecting unpleasant ones. Cultivating what is skillful culminates in practicing the four sublime states so that we can fulfill our potential as caring and compassionate human beings. The Buddha said that cultivating what is skillful *brings benefit and contentment*.

This is our task: to abandon what is unskillful and to cultivate what is skillful. With practice, we can learn to catch desires and painful mental states, such as anger, when they first arise and, knowing that they lead to suffering, choose not to take them up. When these sources of suffering are truly abandoned, our hearts open so wide that we naturally respond to the world as awakened beings—with kindness and friendliness, compassion, appreciative joy, and equanimity.

I trust the Buddha's words, "*If it were not possible, I would not ask you to do it,*" but not because he spoke them. The Buddha said not to rely on someone else's words in place of our own understanding, but instead to investigate and know for ourselves. My own investigation has confirmed that the mind is indeed as soft and pliant as the balsam tree, meaning that we can transform ourselves, even in the face of what appear to be overwhelming difficulties.

Aristotle said: "We are what we repeatedly do. Excellence, then, is not an act, but a habit." Every moment that we abandon what is unskillful, we incline our minds toward abandoning what is unskillful in the next moment. Every moment that we cultivate what is skillful, we incline our minds toward cultivating what is skillful in the next moment.

I've seen this at work in my own life, and I hope you're seeing it in yours. Kindness begets kindness. Compassion begets compassion. Each moment of mindfulness makes it easier in the next moment to catch ourselves before we speak or act in a way that might harm ourselves or others. Each moment we're able to open our hearts and minds to engage our life as it is—being fully present for its joys and its sorrows—is a moment of peace.

By abandoning what is unskillful and cultivating what is skillful, may you awaken in this very life.

Acknowledgments

I extend my heartfelt gratitude to the following:

Lybi Ma, deputy editor, and the other editors at *Psychology Today*, for giving my writing a home on the web. Some of the articles I wrote for *Psychology Today* became seeds for chapters in this book.

Rod Meade Sperry, associate and digital editor of *Shambhala Sun*, for featuring two essays on *Shambhala SunSpace* that became the bases for chapters in this book.

Andy Olendzki and *Insight Journal* for printing in its October 2011 issue an earlier version of the chapter now titled "Looking More Deeply at Suffering and Dissatisfaction."

Josh Bartok, Wisdom Publication's senior editor, whom I've been fortunate to have as the editor for both my books. His wisdom and compassion embody the Buddha's teachings.

Everyone at Wisdom Publications. Wisdom took a chance on an unknown writer and then supported me all the way through this second book. Special thanks to Tony Lulek for always being available to answer my questions; Lydia Anderson for her energy and creativity in promoting the book; and Laura Cunningham for her understanding and diligence, and for her patience with my determination to continue editing until the presses start rolling.

Kari Peterson, who read the manuscript not once, but twice—first as an early draft and again in its final draft form. With a keen and insightful editor's eye, she gave me invaluable feedback from a non-Buddhist perspective. My appreciation runs deep.

Elizabeth Zimmer and Deon Vozov, who spotted copy errors in the manuscript that I'd have sworn were not to be found.

Alida Brill, a writer by profession, who taught me the ropes and whose opinion I value so highly that, when it came back positive regarding a few draft chapters, I knew the project was worth finishing. A year later, she read the manuscript after the major editing had been completed, adding a dusting of gold with her suggestions. I am so grateful that my *How to Be Sick* and her *Dancing at the River's Edge* brought us together.

Dawn Daro, my faithful friend, who enriches my life with her good company and takes my mind off illness and book writing and life's other stresses.

Richard Farrell, my trusted friend, whose intellect and engagement with life keep me sharp, whose common sense keeps me grounded, and whose unwavering willingness to help me and my husband eases my concerns about the effects of my illness on our life.

Sylvia Boorstein, my friend and teacher. She is the Buddha in my life.

Dr. Paul Riggle, my primary care physician, who makes sure I remain (as I like to put it) perfectly healthy even though I'm sick.

The Buddhist discussion group who has been meeting at our house for almost fifteen years. Since becoming chronically ill, I'm not able to participate in a spiritual community away from home but, once a month, that community comes to me: Chuck Yannacone, Jim Schaaf, Joan DePaoli, Sandy Calhoun, Martha Pamperin, Rick Maddock, Lee Hershberger, Sondra Olson, and Lynn Gore. I treasure their wisdom and their company.

The *How to Be Sick* community on the web who come from all over the world—from North, South, and Central America, to Europe, to Russia, to Australia and New Zealand, to East Asia, to Southeast Asia, to India, to Africa, to down the block. Their wisdom is inspiring and their compassion is a comfort.

My children, Jamal and Bridgett Bernhard and Mara and Brad Tyler, who accepted this mysterious illness from its inception and have never made demands on me. I know how rare this kind of support is. The limitations imposed on me by illness can still break my heart, but my children's unconditional acceptance of how I am is a gift from them to me of inestimable value.

My husband, Tony, whose insight into the Buddha's teachings have been invaluable to me, both personally and as a writer. His fingerprints are on many a page of this book. He and I have been partners on the Buddha's path for over twenty years. We've been partners in life for almost fifty. Fifty years of love, friendship, kindness, and compassion. I am blessed beyond measure.

The scholars and teachers who preserved and passed down from generation to generation "the gift that surpasses all other gifts"— the Buddha's teachings.

This book is in memory of Marilyn Wilson
whose brief presence in my life glowed
with the brightness of 10,000 candles.

Bibliography

Aitken, Robert. *The Dragon Who Never Sleeps*
Aitken, Robert. *The Practice of Perfection*
Analayo, Bhikkhu. *Satipatthana: The Direct Path to Realization*
Batchelor, Martine. *The Spirit of the Buddha*
Batchelor, Stephen. *Buddhism Without Beliefs*
Batchelor, Stephen. *Confessions of a Buddhist Atheist*
Beck, Joko. *Nothing Special*
Boorstein, Sylvia. *It's Easier Than You Think*
Boyce, Barry, editor. *The Mindfulness Revolution*
Brach, Tara. *Radical Acceptance*
Brahm, Ajahn. *The Art of Disappearing*
Burch, Vidyamala. *Living Well with Pain and Illness*
Chah, Ajahn. *A Still Forest Pool*
Chödrön, Pema. *The Places That Scare You*
Chödrön, Pema. *Start Where You Are*
Dalai Lama, H.H. *Beyond Religion*
Fronsdal, Gil, translator. *The Dhammapada*
Goldstein, Joseph. *Insight Meditation*
Gombrich, Richard. *What the Buddha Thought*
Gunaratana, Bhante Henepola. *Mindfulness in Plain English*

Halifax, Joan. *Being with Dying*

Hanson, Rick. *Buddha's Brain*

Kabat-Zinn, Jon. *Full Catastrophe Living*

Katie, Byron. *Loving What Is*

Khema, Ayya. *Being Nobody, Going Nowhere*

Kornfield, Jack. *A Path with Heart*

Krishnamurti, Jiddu. *To Be Human*

Lickerman, Alex. *The Undefeated Mind*

Macy, Joanna. *World as Lover, World as Self*

Miller, Karen Maezen. *Hand Wash Cold*

Nhat Hanh, Thich. *Present Moment Wonderful Moment*

Olendzki, Andrew. *Unlimiting Mind*

Richmond, Lewis. *Healing Lazarus*

Salzberg, Sharon. *Lovingkindness*

Seung, Sahn. *Dropping Ashes on the Buddha*

Seung, Sahn. *Only Don't Know*

Stuart, Maureen. *Subtle Sound*

Suzuki, Shunryu. *Zen Mind Beginner's Mind*

Tarrant, John. *Bring Me the Rhinoceros*

Tejaniya, Ashin. *Dharma Everywhere*

Thurman, Robert, translator. *The Tibetan Book of the Dead*

Yeshe, Lama. *Becoming Your Own Therapist*

Index

bodily sensations
  in choiceless awareness meditation
    practice, 105–6
  in five-minute mindfulness prac-
    tice, 98
body scan, 116–17
body scan meditation, 117–20
body sweeping, 114–15
Boorstein, Sylvia, 136, 188, 195
Brahm, Ajahn, 30
brahma viharas. *See* sublime states
  (brahma viharas)
breathing
  awareness of, in mindfulness prac-
    tice, 75–76, 80, 91
  in the body scan meditation, 118
  in five-minute mindfulness prac-
    tice, 96
  in tonglen meditation practice,
    176
Browne, H. Jackson, 149
Buddha, the
  on anger, 59, 164
  awakening of, 2
  on cherishing all living beings, 159
  on dukkha, 27–28, 47
  father, and, 141–42
  on hearing, 97
  on the human condition, 3–4, 9
  on impermanence and change, 10,
    16, 50
  joys and sorrows of, 1
  on labeling the hindrances, 63
  and the marks of experience,
    9–10, 76, 144

on the mind, 39, 162, 167,
  197–98
on mindfulness of the body, 113,
  120
patience, as one of the perfections
  of, 45
on physical sensations, 98
on practice, 4
rebirth and, 24
on seeing, 97
on self-compassion, 174
on skillfulness and unskillfulness,
  209–10
suffering, his exposure to, 141–42
on tanha, 35–36
Buddhadasa, Bhikkhu, 113
Buddhism, traditions of, 4–5
Byron, Lord, 173

C
Campbell, Joseph, 205
catastrophic thinking, 195–96
Chah, Ajahn, 109–10, 197
change, examining, 10–11
Chödrön, Pema, 9, 10, 19, 49, 83,
  137, 167, 189
choiceless awareness as meditation
  practice, 103–4, 105–7
Chuang Tzū, 1
compassion
  accepting others as they are, 156
  as brahma vihara, 137–39, 145
  compassion phrases, crafting,
    172–73
  during meditation practice, 108–9

for oneself, 168–74, 178–79,
182–83, 184
for others, 174–76
intentionally turning the mind to,
203–4
storytelling dukkha and, 53
tonglen meditation practice and,
176–78
complaints and complaint practice,
31–32, 53
control, the impossibility of, 30–31
criticism
and the hindrance of anger, 59
inner critic, 154–55, 161–62,
168–71
curiosity, greeting the day with, 16

D
Dalai Lama, H.H., 43, 50, 111,
162, 168, 179
death awareness practices
author's inspiration to take up,
122–23
death's timing, the mystery of,
126–28
fear, working with, 123–24
goodbye forever, 125–26
grasping, dissolution of, 128–30
mortality, awareness of, 124–25
Denison, Ruth, 65–66
depression, identification with, 20,
21
desire
mindfulness of, 77–78
and the object of desire, 39–40
as source of dukkha, 35–37

the tracing exercise, 53–56
working skillfully with, 40–45
See also tanha (desire)
difficult persons
appreciative joy for, 185
metta practice for, 163–64
dissatisfaction
dukkha as, 27–29, 77–78
recognizing, 31–33
tanha as source of, 45
Dogen (Zen Master), 77
Donizetti, Gaetano, 136
Don't-Know Mind (practice),
153–54
doubt, skeptical *vs.* skillful, 61–62
Draper, Don, 38, 39
dukkha (suffering)
aversion dukkha, 47–49
broken wheel, metaphor for,
32–33, 53
Buddhist concept of, 27–29
complaints as marker of, 31–32, 53
impermanence dukkha, 49–50
storytelling dukkha, 50–56
subtle clues to, 32–33
trying to control, 30–31
See also suffering; *specific types of
dukkha*

E
emotions, weather metaphor for,
191–92
energy, the hindrance of torpor or
lethargy and, 59–60
envy and resentment, working with,
181–84

of thoughts during meditation, 110–11

Jumnian, Ajahn, 39, 41, 192–93, 194

just this, embracing, 78, 83–84, 89, 115, 130

K

Katie, Byron, 31, 89

Khema, Ayya, 52, 64, 123

Khin, U Ba, 114–15, 116

kindness and friendliness (metta)
  accepting others as they are, 156
  as brahma vihara, 135–36
  informal *vs.* structured practice, 165–66
  intentionally turning the mind to, 204
  vs. judgments, 151
  negative judgments, transforming, 155–56
  resistance, handling, 164–65
  structured practice of, 160–64

Kornfield, Jack, 168, 193, 202

Krishnamurti, Jiddu, 103, 104

L

labeling, in the four-step process
  desire, working with, 41, 54
  hindrances, working with, 63, 66, 67, 70
  metta practice, resistance to, 165
  sadness brought about by loss, 172
  let it be, if you can't change it (practice of), 192–95, 205

let it be, in the four-step process
  desire, working with, 43–44
  hindrances, working with, 65, 67
  metta practice, resistance to, 165
  sadness brought about by loss, 172

lethargy. *See* torpor or lethargy

loneliness, practicing with, 89–90, 176–78

loss, compassion for, 171–72

loving your fate, 197–98

M

Macy, Joanna, 24

marks of experience, three
  in choiceless awareness meditation practice, 107
  as common to all human beings, 9–10, 76
  and cultivating wisdom and the sublime states, 144
  the five hindrances and, 57
  impermanence and change, 10–17
  judgment and, 154
  no-fixed-self, 19–25
  and sensory splitting, 115
  suffering or dissatisfaction, 27–33
  See also specific marks of experience

meditation practice
  body scan meditation, 117–20
  choiceless awareness, 103–4, 105–7
  flexibility, 104–5
  tonglen practice, 176–78
  memento mori, 124

metta. *See* kindness and friendliness (metta)

mind

how our minds work, 108

inclination of, importance of, 4, 25, 139, 148, 166, 198

soft and pliant nature of, 38–39, 162, 167, 210

mindfulness

of the body, 113–20

concrete descriptions and, 89–90

and desire, 77

five-minute mindfulness practice, 96–101

gathas and, 92–93

and the hindrances, 78

and impermanence, 11–12, 76–77

mindfulness bell, using, 90–91

multitasking, cutting back on, 86–87

mundane activities and, 81–82

as nonjudgmental awareness, 79

openness to experience and, 83–84

practicing, 75

and self-focused thinking, 80

of sights, 99–100

of sounds, 100–101

storytelling dukkha and, 52

tasks, performing more slowly, 87–89

as tool for cultivating wisdom, 76

Miyazawa, Kenji, 27, 29

moods, weather metaphor for, 191–92

mudita. *See* appreciative joy (mudita)

multiple hindrance attack, 62, 95–96

multitasking, mindfulness and, 86–87

Munindra, 108

N

Neem Karoli Baba, 135

neuroscientists, 4, 19

neutral persons, metta practice for, 163

Nhat Hanh, Thich, 1, 85, 90–91, 92, 153–54, 162

Nietzsche, Frederick, 197

no-fixed-self

in choiceless awareness practice, 107

desire and, 44

and judgment, 152

as mark of experience, 10, 19–25

mindfulness and, 76-77

O

open-heartedness, 2, 4, 29, 53, 120, 133, 173

See also sublime states (brahma viharas)

Orr, Mary, 125

P

patience, 45, 171

Peacock, John, 16–17

perfection as self-expectation, 178

Proust, Marcel, 95, 99

R

rebirth, Buddhist context of, 24

resistance, encountering, 146–47
wisdom and, 144–46
See also specific sublime states
suffering
  and choiceless awareness practice,
    107
  and clinging to self-concepts,
    20–21
  compassion and, 137
  dissatisfaction and, 77–78
  fixed identity as, 22–23, 25
  intensifying via judgment, 152–53
  as mark of experience, 10
  and objects of desire, 42
  relief from, 71
  separation from others as, 23
  in the stories, 43
  tanha as source of, 45
  uncertainty and unpredictability,
    allowing, 13
  See also dukkha (suffering)
Suzuki, Shunryu, 19

T
Taizan Maezumi, 101
The Talmud, 159
tanha (desire)
  acknowledging the presence of,
    39–40, 146
  distinguished from desire for sense
    pleasure, 58
  the "if only" test for, 37–38
  as source of suffering, 35–37, 169
  the tracing exercise and, 53–54
  as want/don't-want, 36–37, 38,
    42, 45

working skillfully with, 40–45
  See also desire
Tarrant, John, 79
Tejaniya, Ashin, 107
ten thousand, meaning of, 1
Thich Nhat Hanh, 1, 85, 90–91,
    92, 153–54, 162
thinking
  the Buddha on, 4
  during meditation practice,
    110–11
  self-focused, mindfulness and, 80
  storytelling dukkha, 50–53, 55,
    90, 114, 177
  thoughts, proliferation of, 80–81
Thurman, Robert, 128–29
tonglen meditation practice,
    176–78
torpor or lethargy, 59–60
tracing exercise, 53–56
Twain, Mark, 196

U
uncertainty and unpredictability,
    12–14, 15–17
unskillfulness, abandoning, 209–11

W
Whitman, Walt, 133, 156, 194
wisdom
  of choiceless awareness, 107–8
  cultivating, 76–77, 205
  greeting the day with, 16
  meaning of, in Buddhist philoso-
    phy, 9

About the Author

Toni Bernhard is the acclaimed author of *How to Be Sick*, a *Spirituality & Practice* "Best Spiritual Books of 2010" winner, and winner of two Nautilus Awards. She's been interviewed on radio across the country and internationally, and she is a regular contributor to *Psychology Today* online. She maintains a personal relationship with her many thousands of fans on Facebook.

Toni fell ill on a trip to Paris in 2001 with what doctors initially diagnosed as an acute viral infection. She has not recovered. In 1982, she'd received a J.D. from the School of Law at the University of California, Davis, and immediately joined the faculty where she stayed until chronic illness forced her to retire. During her twenty-two years on the faculty, she served for six years as Dean of Students.

In 1992, she began to study and practice Buddhism. Before becoming ill, she attended many meditation retreats and led a meditation group in Davis with her husband.

She lives in Davis with her husband, Tony, and their hound dog, Rusty. Toni can be found online at www.tonibernhard.com.

About Wisdom Publications

Wisdom Publications is dedicated to offering works relating to and inspired by Buddhist traditions.

To learn more about us or to explore our other books, please visit our website at www.wisdompubs.org.

You can subscribe to our e-newsletter or request our print catalog online, or by writing to:

Wisdom Publications
199 Elm Street
Somerville, Massachusetts 02144 USA

You can also contact us at 617-776-7416,
or info@wisdompubs.org.

Wisdom is a nonprofit, charitable 501(c)(3) organization, and donations in support of our mission are tax deductible.

Wisdom Publications is affiliated with the Foundation for the Preservation of the Mahayana Tradition (FPMT).